SIGNALS
at the
CROSSROADS

OTHER BOOKS
BY GILBERT W. STAFFORD

Theology for Disciples
Living as a Redeemed People: Studies in James and Jude

SIGNALS
at the
CROSSROADS

GILBERT W. STAFFORD

Foreword by David L. Sebastian

Warner Press

Anderson, Indiana

Coordinator of Publishing & Creative Services
Church of God Ministries, Inc.
PO Box 2420
Anderson, IN 46018-2420
800-848-2464
www.chog.org

To purchase additional copies of this book, to inquire about distribution, and for all other sales-related matters, please contact:

Warner Press, Inc.
PO Box 2499
Anderson, IN 46018-2499
800-741-7721
www.warnerpress.org

All Scripture quotations, unless otherwise indicated, are taken from New Revised Standard Version Bible, copyright 1989, Division of Christian Education of the National Council of the Churches of Christ in the United States of America. Used by permission. All rights reserved.

Scripture quotations marked KJV are taken from the Holy Bible, King James Version.

Cover design by Mary J. Jaracz
Text design by Mary J. Jaracz
Editing by Joseph D. Allison and Stephen R. Lewis

ISBN-13: 978-1-59317-544-3

Printed in the United States of America.
LSI

DEDICATION

Dedicated to the students, faculty, and staff
at the School of Theology at Anderson University
in whose company Gil walked
from August 1976 through March 2008

—Darlene Stafford

Table of Contents

BOOK 2: VISION FOR THE CHURCH OF GOD AT THE CROSSROADS

BOOK 3: SIGNALS AT THE CROSSROADS

FOREWORD

For thirteen years I occupied an office next to Gilbert Stafford. I knew him as a loving colleague, mentor, and friend in the ministry of the gospel. His lifelong work in both the church and academy demonstrated a commitment to scholarship, spirituality, and service. During the last months of his life, it was difficult to see his energetic walk come to a halt and his strong voice reduced to a whisper. But to the very end of his life, literally, he was thinking, planning, and praying about the things that he held most dear. We still miss him.

Gil Stafford loved many things. If you had the privilege of listening to him teach and preach, you knew of his love for the church. He represented the Church of God at many venues, including the Faith and Order Commission of the National Council of Churches of Christ in North America. He practiced what he preached by "extending his hand in fellowship to every blood washed one." He never grew tired of lifting up the ideals of the Church of God reformation movement wherever he traveled.

It should come as no surprise that even in his last months on earth he was working on a third book in his Crossroads series. The first two books in the series, *Church of God at the Crossroads* (2000) and the *Vision for the Church of God at the Crossroads* (2002), helped provide a rich conversation among leaders both in North America and around the world. In 2007, Gil began working on a third book in the series titled *Signals at the Crossroads: The Church of God in the 21st Century.*

I was privileged to read early drafts of the first two books in the series, but the reading of this third partial manuscript was different. When Gil's wife, Darlene Stafford, allowed me to read the outline and two chapters of the new book, the experience was like reading a message sent from the church above to the church below. It was as if I had reengaged in conversation with my departed friend.

In *Signals at the Crossroads*, Professor/Pastor Stafford invites us to come together once again for a church-wide conversation about the future of our life together. In typical Gil Stafford style, this third book in the series welcomes us all into a hallelujah conversation celebrating what God is doing in the church. This new theological conversation calls us to affirm our roots while at the same time exhorts us to remember we no longer live in the nineteenth or twentieth centuries but rather in the twenty-first century with all its promises and pitfalls.

I encourage you to read and reflect with other colleagues on these chapters outlined by Dr. Stafford. When you do, you will begin to share past memories, discuss the suggested "signals" at the crossroads, and renew your hope for the Church of God in the twenty-first century. When we have such ongoing conversations, we honor the intentions of Gilbert Stafford, and more importantly, I believe, the Lord of the church will be well pleased.

David Sebastian
December 2010

PUBLISHER'S PREFACE

The late Dr. Gilbert W. Stafford continues to exert a significant influence over the Church of God movement. His books *Church of God at the Crossroads* and *Vision for the Church of God at the Crossroads* have remained in print for more than a decade and are required reading for ministerial candidates in several states.

Dr. Stafford began work on a third volume in the Crossroads series just before his death in 2008. His family has graciously granted permission for us to include what he had written for that third book with this updated compilation of the first two.

The preface to the third ("Signals") volume is excerpted from a letter that Dr. Stafford gave us shortly before his final illness. He completed a chapter comparing the Church of God in the nineteenth and twenty-first centuries, and outlined a chapter on "Hallelujahs at the Crossroads." However, he was able to flesh out only part of that second chapter, so we are including the portion he finished as well as his list of other trends that he saw as reasons for celebration.

Finally, Dr. Stafford's last chapel address at the Anderson University School of Theology appears as an Afterword to this combined volume. We believe every minister and ministerial student should heed his inspiring exhortation to live holy and blameless before God as we minister in the kingdom.

BOOK 1

CHURCH OF GOD
at the
CROSSROADS

DEDICATION

To my parents, Orell and D. C. Stafford; aunt and uncle, Jesse and Audrey Hatchel; and maternal grandparents, Cora and John Smith, who lovingly nurtured me in the life of the one universal church, and in the life of one particular fellowship, which, I am grateful, wears the scriptural name Church of God.

ACKNOWLEDGEMENTS

I am grateful to the following persons who read the first draft of this small book and offered many helpful suggestions. They asked questions, raised issues, and spoke words of encouragement that guided the writing of the final product, though I alone take full responsibility for all that is said here. Thanks to my seminary colleagues James Lewis, Sharon Clark Pearson, and David Sebastian; and to other colleagues in ministry Jeannette Flynn, Edward Foggs, James Lyon, Robert Pearson, Harold Phillips, Ann Smith, and Nathan Smith. I am grateful for the perceptive responses of my family: to my wife, Darlene; to our son Josh, who is preparing for ministry; to my brother Rod, who is an exemplary pastor; and to my father and stepmother, D. C. and Arietta Shock Stafford, longtime ministers in the Church of God.

INTRODUCTION

As I begin this writing I am sixty years of age[1]. I have been wrestling with the temptation to suppress what I have to say. I could simply continue to enjoy the enriching friendships I have in the church, pursue my work as a preacher of the gospel and teacher, and let others think and talk about where the Church of God now is and where it is going. But I am increasingly convinced that to do so is for me to deny who I am in God's economy. I have decided that I need to express my perspective so that it can be part of the discussion now going on.

I was born in the womb of the church. Both my maternal and paternal grandparents were associated with the Church of God. A granduncle was a Church of God pastor; Grandfather Stafford was a lay preacher loosely related to the Church of God; and my father, a pastor in the church for many years. My stepmother is a longtime minister in the church. One of my brothers is a Church of God minister, and one of our sons is preparing for ministry. I have served as pastor of two Church of God congregations and as speaker on the church's international radio program. Since 1976, I have taught in the church's seminary. In the course of my ministry, I have served on numerous committees and task forces, have represented the church in ecumenical settings, and have preached and taught in numerous settings. I am grateful for the opportunity to have written books used broadly in the church and to have led international doctrinal discussions. The church is my life, and I care deeply about it. For me to say nothing at this point in my life pilgrimage feels too much like wasting who I am as a person.

So, I speak.

---

1. Dr. Stafford died in 2008 at the age of sixty-nine.

Churches, like individuals, change over time and, like individuals, are faced with decisions at various critical points as to which path to follow. Individuals make decisions about their personal identity; they often change and become something that earlier they had no idea of becoming.

Most of us, if not all of us, come to crossroads in life when we decide to go one way instead of another. For example, people ask themselves questions like: Am I going to be a single person or a married person? Am I going to move to a particular place and become a part of that culture? Am I going to be a homeowner or a renter? The decisions we make at such crossroads determine much about our future. Churches, too, come to crossroads when they decide to go one way instead of another.

The focus of what I have to say does not have to do with crossroads pertaining to organizational and structural issues. We have been dealing with those matters for the last decade. We came to the crossroads, made our decisions, and are now moving on with the decisions we made. And I, for one, say, "Hallelujah! Let's move on." The focus of what I have to say has more to do with what might be called Church of God culture. A culture is the way people live together. When we speak of adapting to the culture of a place, we are referring to the things people value, the way they talk, their habits, their way of doing things. Anderson, Indiana, where I now live, has a culture that is different from the culture of my birthplace in Portageville, Missouri. Over the years I have lived in many different cultures: Deep South, lower Midwest, upper Midwest, New England. Each has its own distinctive culture. Just as different places have different cultures, so do different church groups. This book is about cultural issues. It is about the way we live together, our values, and the language of our faith. It is about the way we go about being the church.

Much of this material has been presented in numerous settings, including local churches, state assemblies, and other discussion groups. I am particularly appreciative to the Oklahoma Assembly of the Church of God for providing me the opportunity, in its 1999 Visioning Conference, to begin organizing it.

I share it now in a new format in hope that it may make some small contribution to our church life as we make decisions about how we will be the church in the twenty-first century.

Section One:
Challenges at the Crossroads

CHALLENGE 1: SELF-UNDERSTANDING

CHALLENGE 2: CONGREGATIONAL AUTONOMY

CHALLENGE 3:ANTICREEDALISM

CHALLENGE 4: BEHAVIORAL CODES

CHALLENGE 5: CONSUMERISM

CHALLENGE 6: WORSHIP

CHALLENGE 7: MINISTERIAL CREDENTIALING

CHALLENGE 8: MOBILITY

CHALLENGE 1

Self-Understanding

One of the critical challenges facing the Church of God has to do with its self-understanding. Does it understand itself to be a movement, an association of local churches, or a church fellowship? Deeply ingrained in our way of talking is movemental language. I remember as a teenager being at an international youth convention when a guest preacher referred to us as a denomination. When we all laughed, he was flustered. He amused us because he did not use our language. At the next service he told us he had been informed that the Church of God was not a denomination but a movement. He corrected himself, and all of us were happy because he used the term that sounded good to our ears. He used the right rhetoric.

It is easy for us to forget that *movement* is neither a biblical nor a theological word. It is a sociological word. To use it correctly we need to be in touch with its sociological meaning. In short, a movement is a group of people within a larger whole who are so motivated to bring about change in that larger whole that they are willing to commit themselves sacrificially to bringing it about. A movement organizes itself for the singular purpose of bringing about change. Members of movements share a common vision. They try to influence others to join them because they are convinced of the critical importance of what they are doing. Movements strategize and restrategize for reaching their goals. This willingness to restrategize grows out of their conviction that what they are about must succeed. As a result, movements are characterized by a dynamism that excites people.

Movements, as I have just described them, may be, for instance, political or religious; they may have to do with changes in the social structures of a society (the civil rights movement, for example), or in the spiritual life of churches (the charismatic movement, for instance). Depending on one's point of view, some movements are bad; others, good. Calling ourselves a movement does not determine whether we have God's blessing. Furthermore, it is outsiders, not insiders, who know whether a group is a movement. Movements, by their very nature, make waves in the larger whole that lead outsiders to call them movements. I personally know of no current example of people outside our ranks calling the Church of God a movement, except those who, like the preacher at the youth convention, out of courtesy use the rhetoric we prefer.

If outsiders are not calling us a movement, what, then, are we? Are we simply a loosely connected association of independent congregations, or are we truly a church fellowship? A loosely connected association of independent congregations consists of local churches that have almost nothing in common except perhaps one or two things. As I think about the Church of God, I ask what I can assume about a congregation merely by the fact that it is listed in the *Yearbook of the Church of God*. If a congregation is listed there, can I automatically assume that it is organized in a particular way? No, I cannot. Can I assume that the congregation is taught that all believers are called to the life of entire sanctification? No. Can I assume that it supports Church of God Ministries? No, I cannot. Can I assume that hymns and songs of the Church of God heritage are used from time to time? No. Can I assume that it practices footwashing? No, I cannot. Can I assume that it accepts women in ministry? No. Can I assume that it maintains an open-door policy toward all races and cultures? No, I cannot. Can I assume that it uses Church of God Sunday school materials? No. Can I assume that its pastor knows something about Church of God history? No, I cannot. Can I assume that it has a Trinitarian view of God? No, not even that.

What, then, can I assume simply by the fact that I find it listed in the *Yearbook of the Church of God*? About all I can assume with certainty is that it is listed in the *Yearbook*, has been approved by a state or provincial agency for inclusion in the *Yearbook*, probably holds services of worship in a public location, and believes in Jesus Christ as Savior and Lord.

A loosely connected association of churches has nothing more than some basic, bare-bones commonalties like the ones listed above. For these same congregations to function together as *a united church fellowship*, however, means much more than such bare-bones commonalities. It means that, as a church fellowship, these local congregations would have in common a religious culture that is recognizable in each congregation. Other church fellowships provide some examples of what I mean: the every Sunday observance of the Lord's Supper in Churches of Christ, Christian churches, and Disciples of Christ churches; a connectional system for the placement of ministers in United Methodist churches; and an emphasis on the Holy Spirit in Assemblies of God. Other examples are the unique architecture of Orthodox church buildings, the use of the *Book of Common Prayer* in Episcopal churches, and the Mass in Roman Catholic churches. The list could be much longer. Each of these church fellowships has a particular culture that I can count on wherever I may be. If persons tell me that they are going to attend an Episcopal church in a place where I have never been, I already know something about that church without ever having been there. That does not mean that every Episcopal church is an exact replication of every other Episcopal church, but it does mean that even though Episcopal churches come in many varieties, there is an identifiable culture that serves as the basis for the local flavor.

The Church of God is at a crossroads as to whether we are going to be only a loosely connected association of independent churches or a distinctive church fellowship within God's universal church. Do we, as a church fellowship, have anything precious that we hold in common? One might respond quickly: "Of course, it is the saving gospel of Jesus Christ." I fully agree, but so does every other truly Christian church. Do we have any particular contribution that we are convinced God has called us, as a church fellowship, to make to the whole of his church? The evidence decreases year after year that we are truly such an identifiable church fellowship united by common doctrine, practice, mission, ministries, and worship. Instead, increasing evidence points to each congregation doing its own thing and going its own disconnected way in all the areas just mentioned.

One of many possible examples comes readily to mind. It has to do with our hymnody. Since it can no longer be assumed that a congregation knows the heritage songs of the Church of God, it is increasingly difficult to express a common religious culture through singing. By no means is this to suggest that we should limit ourselves to Church of God heritage songs. How impoverished we would be if we did that! It is good to enrich our worship with new and old songs from many other traditions of the Christian faith. While such enrichment is to be encouraged, we also need—if we are to be a functionally united church fellowship—to learn to sing the songs that are unique to our particular religious culture. Only in this way is it possible, when we come together from all sorts of Church of God congregations, to have at least some songs that are common to all of us as the Church of God.

Congregational Autonomy

A second challenge at the crossroads, directly related to the one above, is whether the independent autonomy of the local congregation is our greatest value. The Church of God now places an emphasis on independent autonomy that earlier was not part of our thinking. This more recent emphasis vies for our allegiance over against the traditional emphasis on the mission of the whole church. In the traditional emphasis, each local congregation understood itself as a reflection of the whole reformation movement, so a commonality existed among the congregations in terms of hymnody, doctrinal emphases, codes of behavior, literature, as well as camp meetings and other gatherings. In the traditional view, it was assumed that a local congregation's primary allegiance was to the mission of the movement. The emphasis was on congregational interdependence, mutual support, and common identity and mission. In the relatively new emphasis, it is a matter of congregational autonomy with little or no attention given to the connectional life within the Church of God as a whole.

I see the difference reflected in the degree of participation by area churches in the special endeavors of a local congregation. In reading my daily journal kept throughout 1959, I notice, for example, that when I preached revival services at the Church of God in Ashland, Illinois, the late Bishop Benjamin F. Reid, at that time pastor of a congregation in nearby Springfield, attended, along with his wife and son, three of the five nights. On at least one night they brought other church members. What took place in the Ashland church was thought of as being more than an Ashland event; it was a Church of God reformation movement event that gave concrete expression to our understanding of biblical unity. Examples of such unity are few and far between these days. One of the factors contributing to this reality is that we tend to think in terms of the local congregation as an entity in and of itself with neither a responsibility for nor connection with other congregations.

Perhaps the most disconcerting personal experience that I have had in this regard in recent years was the time that a member of the Mass Communications Board of the Church of God offered local pastors tapes of what is now known as CBH: Christians Broadcasting Hope.[1] It was an invitation to consider supporting the program in their respective local areas. Most of the pastors graciously received the tapes. One, however, upon taking it, promptly threw it into a wastepaper basket as he lamented with the question, "What has that got to do with my local church?"

Why are we faced with this new spirit of independent autonomy? I think that in some cases it is the outgrowth of an independent spirit that simply wants to be left alone. It is a caving in to the spirit of the times that wants little or nothing to do with anything that is not local. In these cases, it is a spiritual problem that ignores the strong biblical emphasis on the interconnectedness of the people of God. The church in the New Testament is a covenant community—in covenant with God and in covenant with all of God's people.

In other cases, however, congregational independence is the result of either geographical or cultural isolation. If, for instance, a congregation finds itself frozen out of the wider fellowship, it may have few options other than going it alone, and, in the course of years, it develops a style that carries on in that mode even after the initial isolation no longer exists. In these cases, local autonomy is a sociological matter. The issue, of course, is whether it changes into a spiritual problem once the original sociological factors change.

In still other instances it is a matter of practical necessity. The larger body of churches very much wants every congregation to be involved, but that larger body lacks vision. It is stuck in the

---

1. The weekly English broadcast is now known as CBH *ViewPoint*.

ruts of the past and despises anything that is progressive, creative, forward-looking, and new. For a local congregation to cave in to the lethargy of the larger body would be for them to lose their soul as the people of God, and so they strike out on their own, quite independent of the larger body. They may indeed maintain a formal relationship with the larger body for historical and legal reasons but are on a very different wavelength when it comes to Christian mission and sense of identity. In this case, independent autonomy is a missional necessity for the sake of the gospel. But in these cases, also, the biblical emphasis on interconnectedness calls all parties (the larger associations and the congregations) to address the issues leading to the practical necessity.

The Church of God has many examples of congregational independence, some the result of spiritual matters, some the result of sociological matters, and some the result of missional matters. Regardless of the reason, the sense of being part of a unified Church of God with a common mission is missing.

CHALLENGE 3

Anticreedalism

A third challenge at the crossroads has to do with our historic position of being anticreed. In the words of the song "The Church's Jubilee" by Charles Naylor, "The day of sects and creeds for us forevermore is past." Naylor was speaking out against the use of creeds as legalistic barriers between Christians. Naylor's phrase has become a slogan among us. The problem with slogans is that they do not say everything that needs to be said about an issue. They simply grab people's attention and communicate an immediate impression. Naylor and others, by using phrases that we have turned into slogans, were addressing a particular issue, namely, that God is not pleased with legalistic divisions among Christians. I say "Amen" to that; however, such sound bites are nowadays misused in a way that neither Naylor nor others intended. In some conversations in which I have heard Naylor's words quoted, the impression given is that the Church of God is a collection of freethinkers, each of whom believes whatever seems good to him or her. In light of this, everybody else, then, ought to be accepting of whatever others come up with. That way of thinking, however, is not an accurate portrayal of what early leaders of the Church of God had in mind. They very much cared about right doctrine. In fact, most of their writing, teaching, and preaching was explicitly doctrinal. In their view, the doctrinal positions taken by individual Christians, preachers, and congregations were crucially important to the well-being of the church. During those earlier years, when the Church of God was much smaller and more intimate, it was easier to informally maintain purity of doctrine than it is today.

A new challenge presents itself. We have been growing numerically and attracting more people who come to us for strictly practical reasons, such as proximity and program offerings—and let us be glad they come! But it is in this very different historical context that some misinterpret our traditional anticreed stance to mean that we as the Church of God are not called to confess what we believe. The attitude taken by some is that it does not matter what one believes so long as one is nice. This has resulted in a doctrinal drift that in some cases has crossed even the line of what it means to be Christian. I have in mind such basics as belief in the Trinitarian God, belief in Jesus Christ as the only sufficient means of salvation, and the Bible as the written Word of God. Does it matter whether the Church of God confesses its faith on these basic matters? Some among us answer that it does not matter. They sometimes forget that the Church of God came into existence first and foremost as a doctrinal movement. From the very beginning, it did its doctrinal work on the basic assumption that Christians do indeed believe in the Trinitarian God, the full divinity and full humanity of Jesus Christ, the sole sufficiency of Jesus Christ for salvation, and the Bible as the written Word of God. Such matters were not the focus of the writing, teaching, and preaching of the early leaders of the Church of God because they assumed them as being the basics of the Christian faith. It was on this assumed foundation, then, that they pursued their vigorous preaching and publishing work on other matters such as the church, unity, the kingdom, healing, eschatology, salvation, sanctification, and personal holiness.

As we find ourselves at the crossroads, we are challenged to decide which way the soul of the church will go. As I see it, we have several paths from which to choose:

We could take the path of *doctrinal drift* and let happen whatever happens. Whatever doctrinal influences happen to gain ascendancy is quite all right with us. We shall simply float with every wind of doctrine that blows among us.

Another path we could take is that of a *rigid legalism* that freezes our understandings at some point in the church's history and disallows growth and development.

I believe, however, that there is another path that we can take. It is the path by which we would

- overtly confess the historic faith of the Christian church
- commit ourselves to the serious study and preaching of the Word
- be good stewards of the particular understandings that we believe God has entrusted into our care as the Church of God.

If we choose to do so, we can walk this path with love for all others of "like precious faith" (2 Peter 1:1 KJV) concerning the basics of Christianity regardless of whether they agree with us on all other matters. We can walk it as people who are in touch with who we are historically. We can walk this path in communion with all of God's people, regardless of whether they live in our particular tent. We can walk it with confidence, with integrity, and with hospitality toward those with whom we differ on issues other than the basics. We can walk this path with the earnest desire to grow in our understanding of the faith and with the willingness to change as we grow. We can take this path if we choose.

CHALLENGE 4

Behavioral Codes

The fourth challenge at the crossroads has to do with the breakdown of shared behavioral codes. Over the years we in the Church of God have been accustomed to church life in which we hold a commonly shared code of behavior. Nowadays, however, a new attitude exists among us that is similar to the attitude toward doctrine, namely, that each person's behavior is that person's business—and no one else's. This new attitude is liberating in contrast to a rigid prescriptiveness that monitored every moment and action of one's life. In former days our emphasis on behavioral standards could be, and too often was, oppressive, legalistic, and judgmental. Thank God, we are for the most part beyond that, and I hope that we shall never return to it. But now we face another challenging question: Is there any sense in which we share some common understandings as to how we are to live together as a community of faith? The church that pays no attention to the issue of shared behavioral codes of conduct will probably end up with dysfunctional differences among individual church families. When this happens the possibility of being a community of faith is less likely; it is more likely that the *community* will be replaced by a mere *collection* of individuals who have faith.

Most Christian parents make peace with the fact that a difference exists between behavioral standards maintained at home and those in public schools. In this case parents simply say that the difference is between Christian standards and secular standards. Of course, the parents who insist on higher standards run the risk of being viewed as "old fogies" by their children, but that is par for the course. Most Christian parents can weather those kinds of storms. The storm intensifies, however, when not only are the parents out of step with the school but with the church as well. When the behavioral standards insisted on by parents are not shared and reinforced by the church, then the children very well may be convinced beyond doubt that their parents are the old fogiest of old fogies, and the battle is almost always lost.

When I was growing up, the church reinforced the behavioral standards in my home (granted, my father was the pastor, but I think that this was the case in most of our families), and the home reinforced the standards preached and taught at church. Furthermore, the behavioral standards in one family were shared by other families in the church, and the standards of one congregation were very much the same as in other congregations. Such shared behavioral patterns, however, are now in the process of breaking down. Of course, in former days there were always examples of transgressions of the code, but that is just the point: they were viewed as *transgressions* of the code, not simply as *different codes*. When we try to function without a communal code of behavior, the result is that every person, every family, every congregation is left to its own code-making process. What often happens is that we end up either merely reflecting the behavioral patterns of the culture around us or we adopt a behavioral pattern that satisfies our own desires irrespective of Christian values.

I recognize how complicated it is to develop a communal pattern of behavior; however, to give no attention to it is to guarantee the loss of community. Just as a household cannot function as a community apart from some basic behavioral expectations, neither can a church, whether at the local level or at other levels. Without some basic behavioral standards, we become little more than a collection of people instead of a community.

One Church of God pastor of a growing church has observed that such behavioral codes are best communicated in the preaching/teaching ministry of the church. He tells about a man who had been coming to his church for about three years and had been a Christian for about a year and a half. The man testified recently about the changes in his behavioral patterns over that period of time. He said that before he had begun attending that church he had created his own behavioral code. But as he began to listen to the biblical preaching he found that almost every week he was discovering some behavior that he needed to change, sometimes by quitting something and sometimes by beginning something. The preaching was not first and foremost about an arbitrary list of dos and don'ts; rather, it was first and foremost about the message of Scripture. This consistent preaching of Scripture formed a solid basis for the behavioral changes that he began making in concert with the rest of the congregation. He discovered, not on the basis of rigid legalism but on the basis of the loving, consistent, and faithful proclamation of the Word, that behavior does matter.

CHALLENGE 5

Consumerism

The fifth challenge at the crossroads has to do with consumerism. Consumerism gives the highest priority to the wants and desires of the purchaser and consumer of a product. The aim is to make a profit. In order to do that, consumer desires become paramount. The goal is not necessarily the well-being of the consumer; the goal is to get from the consumer something you want (usually money) by giving the consumers what they want. If the consumer seems displeased with the product, the product is changed in order to get more consumers to buy it.

Consumerism has made a tremendous impact on the North American church. This is very understandable because the people who are in the church are the same people who live, move, and have their being in a consumerist culture. It is natural for them to expect that the church also should operate with the same values as the consumerism of the shopping mall.

Actually, I think that the contemporary church in North America has been both afflicted and blessed by consumerism. It is afflicted whenever its ministry is determined by what will sell in the marketplace of religion. If what the church has to sell in the religious marketplace is "not going over the way the church wants it to," the church either eliminates or changes it so that it will "sell." By attending to the consumer mentality, the church tends to shape the gospel in the image of the likes and dislikes of consumers, in which case the gospel is distorted. Not only does consumerism tend to dictate what is offered in the church market, it also tends to lead to competition between churches, much like that between grocery stores. A church wants its volume of business to be greater than the volume of business down the street, and so it packages its products with that in mind. Churches add, subtract, multiply, and divide their religion products primarily for the purpose of outdoing the competition. It is unlikely that many earnest prayers will be offered for the success of another church with which one's own is in competition. Such consumerism is a cancer in the body of Christ.

Consumerism can have some benefits for the life of the church. The consumer mentality reminds us that people should not—and for the most part will not—put up with shabbily presented Christianity. That is good, and the church benefits when it gets in touch with this modern reality. Another value is that consumerism reminds us that we ought to be concerned about connecting with the world for the sake of the gospel. The successful business at the mall is always trying to put its best foot forward. Just so, the church should always be committed to putting its best foot forward so that it can communicate the gospel to more and more people. Also, consumerism reminds us that the church is to be in the public arena with the gospel. A store may have a wonderful product but falter in its sales because of a poor location. Not many department stores will succeed by locating on the back roads of the county. The key is location, location, and location! The point of having a hardware store, for instance, is not so that the employees can enjoy being together in a nice building with good products. The point is to sell the products, and to do that they have to be in areas of high traffic, wherever that is. Consumerism reminds us that the church, too, needs to be in the public arena with the gospel, not out by itself enjoying its facilities and products.

Our challenge is that of functioning with sensitivity to the environment of consumerism without becoming consumer-driven churches. Can we learn the lessons of a consumerist culture without becoming the church of the consumers instead of the church of God?

CHALLENGE 6

Worship

The sixth challenge is that of changes in worship. I think of a pastor who led his congregation into the establishment of two distinctively different forms of worship in an attempt to fulfill the preferences of his congregation. Upon assessing the results, he said: "I came to realize that the congregation has more than two preferences; it has as many preferences as there are people in the church." The church in general in North America is at the present time dominated by worship preference discussions, arguments, and divisions. The Church of God is no stranger to this cultural reality.

In North America at the present time I see several broad approaches to worship. The first is that of worship as *the presentation of a program up on the stage.* The congregation comes to watch and to listen to the program much as one goes to see a play, listen to a concert, or watch a sports event. People who come evaluate the program and if they do not like it, they may simply go to another production that they like better. The aim of the service is to receive the approval of the people who attend. Worship leaders want people to say: "That was a fantastic service." This is productionism.

Another approach is that of worship as *an emotional high.* The sought-after goal is that one feels better at the end of the service. Everything in the service is focused on how people feel. Worship leaders want people to say, "Wow! That was a great feeling. Let's do it again." This is emotionalism.

Yet another approach is that of worship as *a weekly ritual.* Satisfaction is gained by doing the same things the way they have always been done. Worship leaders want people to say, "Thanks for not rocking the boat." This is traditionalism.

An additional approach is that of worship as *a time for getting a religious* "quick fix" *for the week ahead*. This kind of worship gives people enough help to make it through another week but not the transformation of persons from the life of sin to the life of salvation. The unfortunate thing about the quick-fix approach is that when people no longer want a quick fix, they very likely will stop the weekly trek to church before they experience true healing of the soul. Worship leaders who take this approach want people to say, "I got an idea for solving my problem." This is a superficial, quick-fix approach to worship.

In each case, positive evaluations can be made. **It is good to do whatever we do well; it is good to feel joyous in the presence of God; it is good to honor the past; it is good to find in the household of faith solutions to our problems.** Nevertheless, all four of these approaches have some built-in problems. In *productionism*, attention is on the up-front people instead of on God. In *emotionalism*, it is on us instead of on God. In *traditionalism*, attention is on the past instead of on God. In the *quick-fix approach*, it is on solutions to our problems instead of on God.

Other developments on the worship scene are much more encouraging. **One is the renewed emphasis on holy tradition blended with the surprises of the Holy Spirit.** In this approach, one finds an emphasis on both the old and the new. In these services, the congregation is enriched both by familiar tradition and by the unfamiliar surprises of the Spirit.

Another encouraging development in some quarters is the renewed emphasis on both the preaching of the Word and the celebration of the Lord's Supper. At times in the long history of the Christian church, the Lord's Supper has been emphasized at the expense of the preaching and teaching of the Word of God. At other times, the preaching of the Word has crowded out sitting at table with our Lord. The Word, according to 2 Timothy 3:16, teaches, reproves, corrects, and instructs in righteousness. The Supper makes us aware of the nature, cost, and promise of our salvation. Christ's disciples are both to sit at his feet, learning from him, and to recline at his table, communing with him.

Yet another encouraging development is the blending of praise and adoration with information and instruction about God whom we adore. It sometimes happens that worshipers are singing repetitive songs and adoration to God without being instructed as to what kind of God they are praising. This problem is being addressed in many places today in that congregations not only sing praise, adoration, and devotion to God but they also sing about the kind of God this is. Furthermore, the emphasis on Scripture and on biblical preaching keeps before the congregation who it is they adore. They blend *praise to God* with *theology about God*.

There is a resurgence of desire on the part of many congregations to hear the Scriptures taught. Consequently, in many quarters preachers are giving new attention to exegetical and expositional preaching. In addition, they are preaching biblical theme sermons and are going to Scripture for guidance regarding contemporary issues. Instead of choosing topics or passages merely on the basis of what they think will sell, they are choosing to preach and teach the whole biblical counsel of God. They are preaching with the conviction that we as the people of God are nurtured and matured, judged, converted, and healed by the whole of Scripture being taught responsibly and lovingly.

The Church of God is not immune to the negative developments mentioned above, nor, thank God, is it without examples of the encouraging developments. At the crossroads of the present time, we are challenged by whether our worship life will be influenced more by the first set of problematic developments or by the second set of encouraging ones. Will our worship life become increasingly one of productionism, emotionalism, traditionalism, and/or the quick-fix approach? Or will it be characterized by the blending of holy tradition with the surprises of the Holy Spirit? Will it be characterized by an emphasis on both hearing the Word faithfully preached and communing at the table of the Lord? Will it be characterized by an emphasis not only on adoration singing but also on informational singing and teaching? Will it be committed to the preaching and teaching of the whole biblical counsel of God? The decisions that we make on these matters will, to a very great extent, determine our identity as the people of God in the years to come.

CHALLENGE 7

Ministerial Credentialing

The seventh challenge at the crossroads has to do with inadequate standards for the preparation and credentialing of ordained ministers. As things now stand a church in Oklahoma, for example, can assume nothing about what an ordination in South Carolina means. Oklahoma perhaps does not know what doctrinal questions South Carolina asks, what procedures are followed, nor what standards of preparation are required. And South Carolina does not necessarily know what the standards for ordination in Oklahoma are. Furthermore, neither does the national office know. Each credentialing committee sets its own standards. It is altogether possible for a congregation to call a minister who, although ordained, does not believe in the faith of the historic Christian church. In one state ordination service that I attended, those to be ordained were asked, "Do you believe in the one God?" This question surprised me because it is not the distinctively Christian question. Jehovah's Witnesses, Unitarians, Jews, and Muslims all could have said yes to that question. The distinctively Christian question is whether one believes in the Trinitarian God—Father, Son, and Holy Spirit. No public indication was given that night that these persons being ordained into Church of God ministry did, in fact, uphold that distinctively Christian view of God. To be sure, Christians believe in one God, but that is not what sets us apart as Christians. That which sets us apart is that we are convinced the Scriptures teach the Trinitarian view of this one God.

I once received from one of our older ordained ministers an essay on God in which he had set forth his own version of a Jehovah's Witness view. Yet he is an ordained minister in good standing. In his case, we had failed to deal in the credentialing process with such a basic issue as the doctrine of God. The question, then, is this: When I find a minister's name in the *Yearbook of the Church of God*, can I assume that he or she preaches and teaches the historic Christian faith regarding the Trinitarian God? Evidently not! Something is terribly amiss when this is the case.

Furthermore, it is no longer to be assumed that an ordained minister even understands the historic views of the Church of God movement. I have in mind such matters as holiness, entire sanctification, the kingdom of God, the return of Christ, the nature and unity of the church, the manifestations of Holy Spirit baptism, and the ordinances. I once heard a pastor of one of our churches preach a sermon in which he ridiculed the doctrine of Christian perfection. As I listened to his critique of John Wesley's use of the term, he gave no evidence of having read anything that Wesley had written about the subject. Neither did he give any indication that he was acquainted with Holiness literature on the subject. He was making fun of a doctrine that had brought that congregation into existence and was dealing with it on the same basis that outsiders have often dealt with it—ignorance of what Wesley actually wrote and flippant response to the biblical texts about perfection. Needless to say, there was confusion. The longtime members of the congregation had assumed that a minister whose credentials were with the Church of God would at least understand what historically we have preached and taught about such an important subject. But in this case, the minister had transferred to us from another church tradition, and the credentials committee had given him full standing as a Church of God minister without examining his understanding of historic Church of God doctrinal matters. The havoc in that congregation was largely the result of an inadequate credentialing process.

In some cases, local congregations compound the problem by ignoring the credentialing processes altogether and calling ministers from other church traditions, without giving sufficient consideration to doctrinal matters. Sometimes—certainly not always—the ministers called do not even know about Church of

God perspectives. Though they may be persons of Christian integrity, they sometimes bring with them doctrines that are in conflict with historic Church of God understandings. In the course of time, this often leads to conflict that would have been avoided if the call process had been more thorough.

A few years ago I was asked to preach the ordination sermon for a Presbyterian minister. Consequently, I was apprised of the procedure leading up to the ordination. It included extensive examinations, writing, and studies. At the service itself, I was impressed with the questions asked of her. They were in three sections.

The first set of questions had to do with those doctrinal matters that define the Christian community as such—matters such as the Trinitarian God, the person and work of Jesus Christ, the nature of Scripture, and the doctrine of salvation. These are doctrines that define whether one's way of thinking is in harmony with historic Christian belief. These basic doctrines demarcate the line between those who are committed to historic Christianity and those who are not.

The second set of questions had to do with Presbyterian matters. The credentials committee wanted to make sure that the person being ordained understood Presbyterian history, theology, and church polity. Furthermore, they wanted to know whether she agreed with it. The assumption was that Presbyterian churches deserve to have pastors who understand Presbyterian ways of thinking and doing things. For her not to be sufficiently prepared to function within the Presbyterian family of faith would compound the difficulties that are already inherent in the give and take of human relationships.

The third set of questions had to do with her understanding of the local congregation. They wanted her to declare in public what she thinks of herself as minister in the congregation and what she thinks about the congregation. They asked her about her view of her role and about her view of the nature of congregational life.

As I work closely with the United Methodist Church in relation to students at our seminary preparing for ministry in their churches, I am aware that they, too, monitor these three areas very closely in preparation for ordination. Every four years Anderson University School of Theology has to give an account of itself to the University Senate of the United Methodist Church that we are, in fact, introducing their students to the historic Christian faith. Furthermore, we have to provide United Methodist students with a UMC professor who teaches them UMC history, polity, and doctrine. On a regular basis, UMC representatives contact their students who are enrolled here to make sure that they are learning how to think of themselves as UMC ministers in local congregations. The University Senate makes it very clear to us that students will be ordained by the UMC only as long as they are adequately prepared in these three areas. If the Senate were to find that we are faltering in this role, we would lose our approval for training United Methodist ministers.

I hasten to add that these excellent approaches to the ordination process do not guarantee that no problems exist regarding the beliefs and practices of those who come through these procedures. Of course they do. The advantage of having a good procedure is that when the problems arise, the church has a concrete reference point for adjudicating the issue.

The Church of God in its credentialing process simply is not anywhere nearly as careful in dealing with matters of licensing, ordination, and congregational calling. The result is a chaotic situation that inhibits the church from being all that God wants it to be. It remains to be seen as to whether at this crossroads we will sufficiently address our credentialing crisis. Perhaps we have not yet seen enough chaos to shock us into action.

Mobility

Our eighth challenge is that of mobility in the life of the church. Not only are people moving from place to place, but also those who stay put are leaving home on the weekends and are spending more time on the road. This culture of mobility raises multiple issues for us. One issue has to do with whether we are helping people who move from one location to another to make a transition to a new church home. I once contacted a pastor about a long-term member of his congregation who, because of health problems, had moved to another state to live with her nephew. Since I had her address, I thought that the pastor might like to do a pastoral introduction of her to the nearest Church of God pastor. His response was forthright: "Since she is no longer here, we have no further responsibility." This out-of-sight, out-of-mind approach to those who relocate results in many of our people getting lost in the cracks.

Another issue is that of a church's hospitality to newcomers. Newcomers may be unlike the majority of the congregation. They may talk funny or act funny. They may be from places that we have never been. In this age of easy mobility, the grace of hospitality is especially important. I find that some churches consider themselves hospitable simply because they experience warmheartedness among themselves. While they are warm toward each other, they do not know how to reach out to the stranger among them. I have been in church narthexes where much joviality is taking place among people who know each other well while the stranger in the narthex is completely ignored. Those involved in the jovial conversations experience the narthex as a place of hospitality, but in reality the spirit of genuine hospitality to the stranger is completely missing. This kind of Christian hospitality has to be taught. Most of us do not like to be bothered with strangers, whether inside or outside the church. They threaten our sense of security.

An additional issue is that of teaching people the theology of worship on the Lord's Day so that regardless of where they are on the first day of the week, they find themselves in the company of believers. As Hebrews 10:25 puts it, we should be "not forsaking the assembling of ourselves together, as the manner of some is." Culturally we are on the verge of Sunday being no different than any other day. We are already very far down that road. While it used to be that the special character of Sunday was reinforced by cultural patterns (such as closed stores), these patterns continue to evaporate. The time will soon come, and is almost already here, when one would find it difficult to tell by the activity around town the difference between Tuesday and Sunday. With that cultural piece no longer in place the question is not, How do we change Sunday to the way it used to be? The question is, Does the church have a theology of the Lord's Day that is strong enough to sustain it as a worshiping community on the first day of the week even when all the cultural reinforcements are missing?

The church has a critical decision to make in this area. Do we gather on the first day of the week because our Lord was raised from the dead on that day or simply because the culture in general makes it more convenient to meet then? If it is the latter, then the reason for Sunday worship is fast disappearing. If it is the former, however, as was the case for the early church, then it makes no difference whether the culture in general makes it convenient for us to gather on that day. If it is the resurrection that determines our celebration of Sunday as the Lord's Day, then whether we are at home or on vacation, "the assembling of ourselves together" for the church's weekly Easter celebration continues to be practiced.

One church that I know in a rural area of central Michigan has an increase in attendance during the vacation months because the people of that Christian tradition have a strong theology of the

Lord's Day. Consequently, when the vacationers come in, they do not take a vacation from church. Although the culture in general disregards the Lord's Day, they do not. How different that is for many other Christian traditions including our own. We are on the slippery slide of culturalism. Instead, we need to be on the solid ground of the Lord's Day celebration of the resurrection.

These, then, are eight challenges that I see facing the Church of God at the crossroads. Which path we take on each of these issues will influence significantly what kind of people we will be in the future. In fact, the path that we take might even determine whether we continue being a distinct people in God's economy. Is it time to close the shop, so to speak, as a church fellowship? Should we quit all our attempts to be a church fellowship with a common culture and ministry to the world and to the church at large? Should we give in to the tendency to become little more than a collection of independent congregations? Or does God still have business for us to do as a distinct Christian fellowship within the whole church? How we meet the challenges set forth above will be our answer to these questions.

Section Two:
Opportunities at the Crossroads

OPPORTUNITY 1: A PIVOTAL POSITION

OPPORTUNITY 2: MULTICULTURAL CONSTITUENCY

OPPORTUNITY 3: MINISTERIAL MOBILITY

OPPORTUNITY 4: FLEXIBILITY

OPPORTUNITY 5: WOMEN IN MINISTRY

OPPORTUNITY 6: THE CAMP MEETING TRADITION

OPPORTUNITY 7: REMARKABLE DEDICATION AND
                                CREATIVITY

A Pivotal Position

The Church of God is at the crossroads with many opportunities. In the church world, we hold a pivotal position. As far as I know, we are the only church group in existence that has kindred relationships with the following four families of churches. We are related to Holiness churches, to evangelical churches, to Anabaptist churches, and to ecumenical churches.

The use of these terms requires some definitions. *Holiness churches* are those that came into existence out of the nineteenth-century revival in North America that emphasized heart purity as a work of the Holy Spirit subsequent to conversion. Examples are the Church of the Nazarene and the Wesleyan Church. *Evangelical churches* grew out of the early twentieth-century modification of Fundamentalism. Evangelicalism found the rigidity of Fundamentalism unacceptable. While holding to the fundamentals of historic Christian faith, evangelicals as a whole are cooperative with other Christians, devoted to positive engagement with the academic community, and committed to the evangelization of the world. Billy Graham is the epitome of the evangelical approach. *Anabaptist churches* are rooted in that part of the sixteenth-century reformation in Europe often called the Radical Reformation. They differed from the Lutheran, Reformed, and English segments of the Reformation in that they were convinced that none of the others went far enough. They insisted on the necessity of believer's baptism, following the teachings of Jesus in daily life, and worshiping in a simple manner. Examples of Anabaptist churches are the Mennonite Church and the Church of the Brethren. *Ecumenical churches* are part of a worldwide movement for doctrinal dialogue among the churches. They emphasize cooperative work and make attempts to arrive at mutual understandings and agreements in matters of doctrine and practice. Examples are the United Methodist Church and the Presbyterian Church (U.S.A.).

These four streams of Christianity are, in many respects, very different, and yet the Church of God is connected to all four. Let me illustrate. In relation to Holiness churches, Dr. Barry Callen, former university professor at Anderson University, is the editor of the *Wesleyan Theological Journal*, published by the Wesleyan Theological Society. Furthermore, Dr. Susie Stanley and Dr. Sharon Clark Pearson, two distinguished scholars of the Church of God, have served as officers of the WTS. These two along with Dr. Juanita Leonard and Dr. Christina Accornero, former faculty members of Anderson University School of Theology, are active in the Wesleyan-Holiness Women in Ministry.

In relation to the evangelical churches, Dr. Edward L. Foggs, general secretary emeritus of the Leadership Council of the Church of God, has a long-term association with the National Association of Evangelicals.

In connection with Anabaptist churches, several of us, including Dr. Merle Strege and Dr. Callen of Anderson University, are participants in the Believers' Church Conference, which consists of churches that practice believer's baptism. In 1994 Anderson University School of Theology hosted one of these conferences on the subject of believer's baptism.

In regard to the ecumenical churches, the Church of God has been a member of the Faith and Order Commission in North America since its inception in Oberlin, Ohio, in 1957. In fact, we are the only church group that does not belong to the National Council of Churches of Christ in the USA that has participated in Faith and Order discussions without interruption since 1957. For many years John W. V. Smith was our representative. I served in this capacity. Over the years our curriculum editors have played key leadership roles in the development and implementation of the work of the Committee on the Uniform Series which is part of the education cluster of the NCCCUSA.

No other church group in North America has this particular package of relationships. This, I believe, makes it possible for us to be a pivotal presence in each of these settings. When we are in holiness settings, we can lift up evangelical, believers' church, and unity themes. When we are in evangelical settings, we can lift up holiness, believers' church, and unity themes. When we are in believers' church settings, we can lift up holiness, evangelical, and unity themes. And when we are in ecumenical settings, we can lift up holiness, evangelical, and believers' church themes.

On the local level, often it is only the Church of God pastor who is able to cross these lines and fellowship with associations of churches that are off-limits to others. I know of instances where the Church of God pastor is the only pastor in town who is a member of the evangelical association, the holiness association, and the ecumenical association all at the same time. This grows out of who we are historically. We are holiness people with a passion for unity and a commitment to such practices as believers' baptism and footwashing. We are unity people with a passion for both evangelism and holiness. We are evangelicals who are also committed to holiness of life and the unity of God's people. We are believers' church people who are committed to holiness, evangelism, and unity. Probably no other seminary in the world has the following components in its statement about itself: "As the graduate seminary of the Church of God, Anderson University School of Theology is committed to the biblical essentials of Christian holiness and church unity which have been hallmarks of the movement's message for more than a century. Honoring the entire Christian heritage, Anderson University School of Theology aspires to be biblical in orientation, evangelical in emphasis, and ecumenical in spirit."

OPPORTUNITY 2

Multicultural Constituency

The second opportunity we have at the crossroads is our multiracial, multicultural constituency. Over 20 percent of us are African American. A growing percentage of us are Hispanic. We have a history of German, Greek, and Arabic constituents in North America. We have strong congregations in places as diverse as California and Pennsylvania, Oklahoma and Wyoming, Florida and Massachusetts, Arizona and Ohio, Oregon and Indiana, and Kansas, Washington, and Maryland. We have a presence in every section of the country. We are rural, urban, small town, metropolitan, and suburban.

Given this racial, cultural, and geographical diversity, we have had to attend to issues on a very practical level that for other church groups are merely theoretical. Many people in our churches are attuned to social issues that escape the attention of people in other churches. To be sure, this diversity leads to strain and stress in our relational life. But this strain and stress can lead to resolution as to how we will live redemptively together. And such resolution, in the course of time, leads to maturity. Maturity leads to mutual understanding; mutual understanding leads to mutual enrichment; and mutual enrichment leads to being a sign of the kingdom of God.

In recent years the flame of reconciliation has burned brightly among us. In both the national and the regional venues, great strides have been made on matters of practical reconciliation. This has been exhibited in places such as Mississippi, Georgia, and Virginia where there have been major strides in the merging of assemblies formerly organized along racial lines. It has been exhibited nationally in meetings explicitly called for the purpose of racial reconciliation. At the 1998 Visioning Conference in Colorado, the agenda was changed in order to take into account a groundswell of concern about such matters.

The spirit of reconciliation is also evident in a new spirit of openness between different theological traditions in the church, especially in regards to our self-understanding. Some among us are greatly influenced by leaders such as F. G. Smith, who understood the Church of God to have been prophesied in the book of Revelation. Others among us are greatly influenced by leaders such as C. E. Brown, who discounted the prophetic emphasis and understood the Church of God to be another instance in the long history of radical reformations that, down through history, God has used to purify the church. It is my experience that persons who differ on this issue view each other as being authentic transmitters of the theological heritage of the Church of God. Both traditions are representative of who we are, and those who differ can nevertheless affirm each other as equals in the Church of God.

Likewise, a spirit of cooperation and mutual appreciation exists among the various schools sponsored by the church, instead of a spirit of competitiveness. It is refreshing to experience this atmosphere of mutuality.

OPPORTUNITY 3

Ministerial Mobility

The third opportunity at the crossroads has to do with ministerial mobility (not to be equated with the short-term pastorates of ministers who never put down roots and effect long-term growth). Our ministers move from place to place all over the country. The advantage of this is that it is difficult for any area of the country not to be influenced by the thinking in another area of the country. We have a remarkable cross-fertilization of ideas that makes narrow regionalism less likely. It also provides the environment whereby pastors can learn different approaches, methodologies, and emphases. If they are not flexible, probably they will not make it moving from pastorate to pastorate. Often the paradigms used for pastoral ministry are changed when pastors move to other locations. From time to time I hear pastors who have moved to a different part of the country talking about having to learn new ways of looking at things. Such pastoral mobility also introduces congregations to different ways of thinking and challenges them with new questions and issues. This kind of ministerial mobility makes it more difficult to maintain a narrowly localized mentality. In many church groups most ministers stay in the same general locality during their whole professional life. That tends to lead to strong localisms. Although we certainly have some of that, it is not as prevalent among us.

OPPORTUNITY 4

Flexibility

The fourth opportunity at the crossroads is flexibility. I have observed that we have remarkable flexibility and resilience when it comes to change. The recent shifts in national structure have met with general support and patience. Such sweeping changes in other church groups would have led to major resistance.

I do not mean that we are gullible about change. We do monitor and critique change. We do insist that change, in the end, should work out for the good of the whole. But I am glad to see little indication that the church resists change simply because it is change. The movement embraces change when it is convinced that it is for the good of the whole.

OPPORTUNITY 5

Women in Ministry

The fifth opportunity at the crossroads is our longtime commitment to women in ministry. While other church groups wrestle with this issue, we had the issue settled from the very beginning. Historically, we were informed about this on the basis of the Acts 2 Pentecostal outpouring of the Holy Spirit, in fulfillment of the prophecy of Joel. The prophecy said that as a result of God's Spirit being poured out, "sons and daughters" would prophecy. The Spirit is poured out on both men and women, with no distinction being made as to what one can or cannot do. This understanding of Acts 2 has led both Pentecostal and Holiness churches to affirm that God calls women as well as men into the ordained, preaching, pastoral ministry. Since its inception, the Church of God has understood Acts 2 as definitive of what it means to be the church. Not only have we allowed women in ministry, but we have affirmed and encouraged them. This is not to say that one does not find pockets of resistance to this position. But there is a big difference between a church group that as a whole rejects the idea of women in ministry and a church group that deals with pockets of resistance from the standpoint of a long-term commitment to it.

In the Church of God, women are in ministry, not as the result of the late twentieth-century feminist movement, but as the result of the nineteenth-century Holiness Movement. I note this not to denigrate the positive contributions of the feminist movement but to maintain historical accuracy. Our commitment to women in ministry is not related to a political agenda; instead, it is related to an understanding of both the ministry of Jesus and the outpouring of the Holy Spirit on the day of Pentecost. We are committed to it not for political but for theological reasons.

The Camp Meeting Tradition

The sixth opportunity we have is that of the camp meeting tradition. From the beginning of the movement's life, the camp meeting tradition has provided the opportunity for different congregations to establish intimate relationships across congregational lines. It has provided the opportunity for friendships to form and for supportive relationships to develop. The result of this tradition is that Church of God people have tended to relate to each other not on a merely formal, institutional basis but on an informal, personal basis. Camp meeting provided an environment within which natural families lived together with the church family. It was a place where people from different congregations developed the values of a common spirituality. Over the years, these camp meetings—as well as youth camps, conventions, and conferences—have served as a bonding influence among us.

In many instances, a camp meeting became the mark of one's spiritual identity. It is not unusual to hear persons say something like, "I grew up in the St. Louis camp meeting." They mean that each year, probably from childhood to adulthood, they went to the camp meeting in St. Louis, Michigan. There, friendships, relationships, and understandings were forged that have defined them spiritually. Many of our camp meetings continue to serve as family reunions both for the natural family as well as for the spiritual family.

The camp meeting tradition has, to a very great extent, defined what we mean by church. Church is not an organization that one joins. Church is a gathering in which one participates.

OPPORTUNITY 7

Remarkable Dedication and Creativity

The seventh opportunity at the crossroads is the remarkable dedication and creativity that is part of the character of the Church of God.

I see it in the depth of persistent dedication on the part of pastors and other leaders in small, often struggling, congregations who keep on keeping on because they believe in the historic message of the Church of God. I often bow my head in gratitude for them.

I see it in the holy grit of many who are involved in the arduous task of planting new churches. Thanks be to God for their creative leadership that in many cases has led to the establishment of large, thriving congregations. I often stand in amazement at what has been done.

I see it in the wise and faithful leadership of established churches that are moving into new modes of ministry and witness. What a blessing it is to experience the refreshment of the Spirit in those churches.

I see it in the dedication of persons to missionary service, at great personal cost. I see it in the creative and persistent efforts of persons committed to endeavors such as prayer, peace, social concerns, and the publication of the church's historic literature.

I see it in the attitude of "with God's help we can do it" in every venue of the church's life. I see it in the "let's pool our resources and pull together" attitude when some part of the church family is in crisis.

I see it in the vigorous bridge-building work between different segments of the church. I see it in the eyes of young and old alike who overflow with ideas as to how things could be improved. Praise God for this incredible bundle of divine energy!

In what sense, then, are these opportunities? Let me summarize. We have the opportunity to relate to many different church traditions, to be enriched by them, and, we hope, to enrich them. We have the opportunity to interpret some Christian traditions to others and to help them to appreciate the values of others.

We have the opportunity to demonstrate the reconciling power of the gospel in a multiracial, multicultural fellowship. We are a test case. Will a church like ours eventually break apart? Will we remain in separate rooms, though under the same roof? Or will we be a fellowship of reconciliation, an example of Christ's reconciling love in the midst of the world's and the church's brokenness?

We have the opportunity to be a truly national and international church even though we are a relatively small group. Whereas it is easy for church fellowships to be little more than collections of localized ways of thinking and doing, we have the opportunity to be a church fellowship with a global outlook.

We have the opportunity to demonstrate the balance between continuity and flexibility. Instead of getting off balance either on the side of continuity or on the side of adaptability. We can show the importance of both.

We have the opportunity to give witness to the Spirit of Pentecost that was poured out on the whole church including both young and old, men and women. The Holy Spirit uses both young and old, male and female, for the benefit of the whole. We have the opportunity to show the difference between a merely political, secular egalitarianism, and a Christian, Spirit-prompted egalitarianism.

We have the opportunity to be a church where genuine community is a reality. We can be a worldwide movement in which warmth, intimacy, caring, mutual support, and transformation are the dominant characteristics. We can show the church at large what it is like to be the church in a relational way instead of merely in an institutional way.

We have the opportunity to channel the incredible bundle of divine energy that by God's grace is ours for winning of the lost, for ordering our life together, and for our ministry to the whole people of God.

Section Three:
Possibilities at the Crossroads

POSSIBILITY 1: A GOSPEL TRUMPET CHURCH

POSSIBILITY 2: A "WHAT THE BIBLE TEACHES" CHURCH

POSSIBILITY 3: A "WHERE CHRISTIAN EXPERIENCE MAKES YOU A MEMBER" CHURCH

POSSIBILITY 4: A "PERFECT LOVE" CHURCH

POSSIBILITY 5: A "WE REACH OUR HANDS IN FELLOWSHIP" CHURCH

POSSIBILITY 6: A "KINGDOM OF PEACE" CHURCH

POSSIBILITY 7: A "TOGETHER WE GO TO MAKE DISCIPLES" CHURCH

The church can be considered from at least two points of view. The first is to look at the institutional life of the church from the first century down to the present. As one looks at this history, one finds the development of institutional structures and the emergence of strong leaders. One also finds in church history splits within existing structures and the development of new church structures. In addition, church history includes the accounts of revivals, movements, and reformations; the merging of denominations; and the spread of the church around the world. Church history is the story of the church as it presents itself to the world. It is about the external life of the church.

Several years ago, when Darlene and I were in Tokyo, Japan, riding on a train one Sunday morning, I commented to her that the cityscape looked so different in that we could see no signs of the presence of the Christian church. Then, all of a sudden, on the horizon we saw a steeple with a cross. "Ah!" we said to each other, "that must be where a Christian congregation meets!" If we had not been on our way to a Church of God congregation that morning, we probably would have figured out how to get over to that building because it had the external sign of church. Had we gone there, we probably would have found them reading from the Bible, singing hymns of praise to God the Father, Son, and Holy Spirit, and praying to God in the name of Christ Jesus. All of these are external signs of church.

When we pick up the *Yearbook of the Church of God* and find out where our congregations are located, when they were founded, how many attend the services, and who is on the pastoral staff, we are dealing with the church as it externally presents itself. We could say the same thing about all the church buildings up and down the streets of our towns: Baptist, Nazarene, Methodist, Church of Christ, Church of God (Anderson), Church of God (Cleveland), Presbyterian, Assembly of God, and the list goes on. They are signs of the church as it externally presents itself. Each of these institutions has a history. The histories of all these church fellowships are important resources for writing the history of the Christian church, for all of them have the external signs of being church.

Let us put it another way. If you were in a place where only one of the above churches is located and wanted to worship with other Christians on the Lord's Day, you would likely go to that church even without knowing anything about the people in the congregation. You would do so because it has the external signs of being church.

Important as external signs are, however, they do not guarantee that it is a church that is pleasing to God. For example, the seven churches of the book of Revelation were indeed churches that were not altogether pleasing to God. The same is true of the church at Corinth. This, then, is the second way to think about church: to examine its spiritual qualities to see whether it the church that is pleasing to God.

How can we as the church of Jesus Christ be more pleasing to him than we are? That question has inspired revivals, renewal movements, and reformations throughout history. Our particular fellowship came into existence for the purpose of reforming the church so that it would be more pleasing to God. But the crucial question is: "What kind of church is pleasing to God?"

A Gospel Trumpet Church

First, the church that is pleasing to God is a Gospel Trumpet church. It is a church where the gospel can be heard above all other sounds.

In Galatians 1:6–9, Paul deals with a church that is not pleasing to God because it is not a gospel church. It has replaced the gospel with an emphasis on Jewish legalism. Paul pleads with it to return to the preaching and teaching of the original gospel of salvation. He says: "I am astonished that you are so quickly deserting the one who called you in the grace of Christ and are turning to a different gospel—not that there is another gospel, but there are some who are confusing you and want to pervert the gospel of Christ. But even if we or an angel from heaven should proclaim to you a gospel contrary to what we proclaimed to you, let that one be accursed! As we have said before, so now I repeat, if anyone proclaims to you a gospel contrary to what you received, let that one be accursed!"

Likewise, the sixteenth-century reformation led by Martin Luther was a call for the church to return to being a gospel church. His proclamation that "the just shall live by faith" was a rediscovery of the gospel. Paul in the first century and Luther in the sixteenth were convinced that the only way that the church could be pleasing to God was for it to be a gospel church.

That is our heritage too. We began the Church of God movement with a journal called the *Gospel Trumpet*, and we sing a song with the words, "Salvation's free, glad joy to all of Adam's fallen race / We'll tell the story far and near of saving, keeping grace."[1]

---

1. D. O. Teasley, "A Song of Joy," *Worship the Lord: Hymnal of the Church of God* (Anderson, IN: Warner Press, 1989), no. 615.

A church that is pleasing to God is one in which the predominant sound is that of the gospel. It is true that many other sounds also need to be heard, such as the sounds of good stewardship, right living, the ordinances of the church, and end-times issues, just to mention a few. But nothing must be allowed to drown out the gospel sound—namely the message that God in Christ forgives, sanctifies, and restores us to his image, and does it all by God's grace. The good news is that salvation is the gift of God. When a church allows other sounds to predominate over this one, it gets out of kilter. The gospel must always be a commanding, trumpet-like sound. Is your congregation and mine a Gospel Trumpet church? Is the Church of God as a whole a Gospel Trumpet church where the most commanding sound among us is not our history about the gospel but the gospel itself?

POSSIBILITY 2

A "What the Bible Teaches" Church

Second, the church that is pleasing to God is a "What the Bible Teaches" church. It is a church that studies, teaches, and preaches Scripture, and lives according to its message. Second Timothy 3:14–17 is biblical evidence that even in the first century the church was concerned about this issue: "But as for you, continue in what you have learned and firmly believed, knowing from whom you learned it, and how from childhood you have known the sacred writings that are able to instruct you for salvation through faith in Christ Jesus. All scripture is inspired by God and is useful for teaching, for reproof, for correction, and for training in righteousness, so that everyone who belongs to God may be proficient, equipped for every good work."

John Calvin in his *Institutes of the Christian Religion* expresses his concern for this when he writes: "No man can have the least knowledge of true and sound doctrine, without having been a disciple of the Scripture"(I,VI,2).[2] The importance of the reading, study, teaching, and preaching of Scripture was lifted up in a variety of ways by the sixteenth–century reformation as it took form in Switzerland. One way the Reformers emphasized their commitment to Scripture was to move the pulpit to the center of the chancel in order to remind the people that when they came to church they were to expect to hear the Word of God read and preached. In fact, the preaching garb of ordained ministers in the Swiss part of the reformation was the academic gown worn by professors. This made it visually clear that when

---

2. Hugh T. Kerr, editor, *A Compend of the Institutes of the Christian Religion by John Calvin* (Philedelphia, PA: West Minster Press, 1964), 14.

the preacher went into the pulpit he was supposed to teach the Word of God. This Swiss part of the reformation made its way to other lands, especially to Scotland and later to the United States. In the States, we know this part of the sixteenth-century reformation mainly through the Reformed and the Presbyterian denominations. When ministers from these churches preach, they still wear academic attire. They wear robes like professors in university processions wear because they are considered teachers of the Word of God.

The central pulpit and academic robes are simply ways to exhibit a commitment to the study of the Word of God. It should be obvious, however, that the position of furniture and the garb worn by preachers do not guarantee the centrality of the Word. They simply illustrate it. A preacher, though dressed in an academic robe and preaching from a central pulpit, can, nevertheless, ignore the Word of God. And on the other hand, strong preaching of the Word can and often does take place from a pulpit at the side and by one without an academic robe. The placement of furniture and the clothes worn are not the issue. The issue is whether the church is one that studies, teaches, preaches, and practices the message of the Bible.

This has been the historic commitment of the Church of God. One of our most popular book titles has been F. G. Smith's *What the Bible Teaches*. Also, one of our favorite song phrases is D. O. Teasley's "Back to the blessed old Bible, Back to the light of its word."[3] Our people need solid exegetical and expositional preaching. Exegetical preaching takes a verse or so and peals back the meaning of the words and sentences. Expositional preaching takes a longer text and develops the big ideas set forth in it.

We also need Bible-based doctrinal and Bible-based topical preaching. Doctrinal preaching takes a theme, such as the church, and develops a view of the theme that is informed by more than one passage of Scripture. Bible-based topical preaching deals with

---

3. D. O. Teasley, "Back to the Blessed Old Bible." *Worship the Lord: Hymnal of the Church of God* (Anderson, IN: Warner Press, 1989), no. 354.

a particular issue from a biblical point of view, for instance, "How to Deal with Hurt the Jesus Way."

The Church of God has a long tradition of being a "What the Bible Teaches" church. Regarding this, we are in harmony with the Swiss reformation. Historically, the assumption among us has always been that when we go to church we will receive further biblical instruction. We have a long history of making the major criterion for ordination into Christian ministry the ability to "rightly divide the Word." But as we find ourselves at the crossroads today, this is not always the first and foremost consideration either for ordination or for calling pastors. Sometimes the foremost consideration is that they are good administrators or have a business head on them or are good at pastoral counseling or sing well or relate to people cordially. While each of these is important, if the ordained ministers in our churches are not basically teachers, preachers, and livers of the Word, the church will cease being a place where people are nurtured week after week on the Scriptures.

This means we have to give careful consideration to how we prepare them for this work. First and foremost, we must insist that they be persons with excellent Christian integrity in every area of their lives. While that is basic, more is needed. Being a Christian with warmth of Spirit and integrity of life are not sufficient credentials for being an informed, well-prepared, capable minister of the Word. Unless we attend to this—and soon—we will become little more than a religious society living on our memory of the past, concentrating on keeping the church doors open, and developing programs that we hope people will like, but we will not be known as a fellowship committed to the serious study and application of the Bible's message.

A "Where Christian Experience Makes You a Member" Church

Third, the church that is pleasing to God is one "Where Christian Experience Makes You a Member" church. It is a church where hearts are aflame with God. In Luke 24:32, after the disciples at Emmaus had recognized Jesus in the breaking of bread, "they said to each other, 'Were not our hearts burning within us while he was talking to us on the road, while he was opening the scriptures to us?'"

On May 24, 1738, John Wesley had his own burning heart experience of Christ. In his journal he writes: "In the evening, I went very unwillingly to a society in Aldersgate Street, where one was reading Luther's Preface to the Epistle to the Romans. About a quarter before nine, while he was describing the change which God works in the heart through faith in Christ, I felt my heart strangely warmed. I felt I did trust in Christ, Christ alone for salvation; and an assurance was given me that he had taken away my sins, even mine, and saved me from the law of sin and death."

The burning heart was the experience of the Emmaus disciples. It was the experience of John Wesley, and was the emphasis in the Wesleyan movement. It has been our historic emphasis as well. In our churches a widely used slogan for many years was "Where Christian Experience Makes You a Member." This meant that the test of membership is whether one has come into a personal, heartfelt experience of Jesus Christ. To be a Christian is not merely to know and adhere to all the right doctrines. It is not a matter of joining an organization. It is not a matter of following that organization's. To be a Christian is to know Jesus Christ in such a personal way that one has a testimony to share with others.

One of our songs is Teasley's "I Know in My Heart What It Means." The first stanza says:

When the gospel is preached in the name of the Lord
    By the Spirit sent down from above,
My soul thrills with joy at the sound of His word,
    For I know in my heart what it means.
I know in my heart what it means,
    Salvation, that word so divine;
His Spirit has witnessed to mine,
    And I know in my heart what it means."[4]

This emphasis on personal experience is often expressed in worship by the lifting of a hand in testimony. In contemporary worship expressions, we often raise both hands in praise and adoration of God. That is to be commended. But the "hand of testimony" is also to be commended. The hand of testimony is a way of saying, "I know personally what that song is talking about, and I want to give a witness that I know in my heart what it means." In some settings, people express their witness to the truth by standing as the song is sung or the message is preached.

The church that pleases God is a church where hearts are aflame with God. It is a church made up of people who know God not only with their minds but also with their hearts. Times when people come to personal conversion traditionally have been associated with the use of the public altar rail. In some of our churches, however, the public altar call is no longer a practice. Whether churches have public calls is not, however, the most important issue. The most important issue is whether people are being called to a personal encounter with the Lord. The most important issue is that every person has a testimony of his or her

---

4. D. O. Teasley, "I Know in My Heart What It Means," *Worship the Lord: Hymnal of the Church of God* (Anderson, IN: Warner Press, 1989), no. 417.

heart being aflame with God. When and where that happens is not the crucial issue, but that it happens. If it does not happen, then we will end up being a nice, churchy organization made up of people who may look right, act right, and talk right, but people who do not have a personal walk with the Lord. Such nice churchy people can talk about raising the budget, paving the parking lot, and hiring a new staff person, but they cannot talk authentically about the Lord. They may have lots of religious information about the Bible, about the history of the local church, about doctrinal matters, but they do not have a personal testimony about their relationship with the Lord.

POSSIBILITY 4

A "Perfect Love" Church

Fourth, the church that is pleasing to God is a "perfect love" church. It is a church where people love God wholeheartedly. This idea of perfected love is based on 1 John 4:16–17: "God is love, and those who abide in love abide in God, and God abides in them. Love has been perfected among us in this: that we may have boldness on the day of judgment, because as he is, so are we in this world. There is no fear in love, but perfect love casts out fear; for fear has to do with punishment, and whoever fears has not reached perfection in love. We love because he first loved us. Those who say, 'I love God,' and hate their brothers or sisters are liars, for those who do not love a brother or sister whom they have seen, cannot love God whom they have not seen. The commandment we have from him is this: those who love God must love their brothers and sisters also."

In eighteenth-century England, John Wesley focused on this passage of Scripture as he preached and taught the doctrine of Christian perfection. He was roundly criticized by the people of his own day—and those who continue to teach it often are criticized as well. Wesley's response was that since the idea of perfection is in Scripture we have little choice but to try to understand it and teach it. In response to his critics, he explains in *A Plain Account of Christian Perfection* that it is "purity of intention, dedicating all the life to God. It is the giving God all our heart; it is one desire and design ruling all our tempers. It is the devoting, not a part, but all, our soul, body, and substance, to God." Continuing, he says: "It is all the mind which was in Christ, enabling us to walk as Christ walked. It is the circumcision of the heart from all filthiness, all inward as well as outward pollution. It is a renewal of the heart in the whole image of God the full likeness of Him that created it." Concluding, he adds: "It is the loving God with all our heart, and our neighbor as ourselves" (section 27).

From childhood, Wesley was a member in the Church of England. In that tradition, one of the prayers found in the *Book of Common Prayer* and used regularly in the services of worship is the following. "Almighty God, to whom all hearts are open, all desires, known, and from whom no secrets are hid: Cleanse the thoughts of our hearts by the inspiration of your Holy Spirit, that we may perfectly love you and worthily magnify your holy name: through Christ our Lord. Amen." Wesley asked his fellow church members whether they thought that God could answer that prayer. Can God do such a work in us that we can "perfectly love" God and "worthily magnify" God's holy name? The answer often received to his question was "Yes, of course, there are moments in life when that is the case, but not all the time." Wesley's response was: "If some moments, then why not moment by moment all the time?" Based, therefore, on both the scriptural passage regarding perfect love and this prayer used regularly in his church, he proclaimed unashamedly that God desires to do such a work of sanctifying grace in the hearts of believers that they will, in fact, "perfectly love" God and "worthily magnify" God's holy name, moment by moment.

As we see in one of the quotations above, Wesley connected this love of God with the love for others, as, indeed, 1 John does. Perfect love, then, is to love God wholeheartedly and to love others with this divine love. Perfect love, however, is not to be misunderstood as flawlessness. Instead, as Wesley repeatedly emphasized, it is to be understood as a relationship of wholehearted commitment to God. The thing that drove Wesley was the deep conviction that in order for the church to be pleasing to God it must consist of believers who love God wholeheartedly; this is what it means to be perfected in love.

Wesley's witness to this teaching of Scripture was so stoutly resisted by the Church of England that Wesley's movement, known as Methodism, finally had to function as a separate church fellowship rather than as a movement within the Church of England. Methodism jumped the Atlantic and became well established on American soil. In the course of time, however, many Methodist churches grew cold regarding Wesley's emphasis on Christian perfection. Consequently, in the nineteenth century a revival broke out in American Methodism for the purpose of lifting up the original Wesleyan message about holiness of heart. In the course of time, though, the revival developed into a movement that went beyond the borders of the Methodist Church. This became known as the Holiness Movement. During the latter part of the century, D. S. Warner was deeply influenced by the teachings of this movement. A passage of Scripture often at the center of the movement was 1 Thessalonians 5:23: "May the God of peace himself sanctify you entirely; and may your spirit and soul and body be kept sound and blameless at the coming of our Lord Jesus Christ."

The word in the above passage translated as "entirely" is used only here in the Greek New Testament. It is made up of two words: *holos*, meaning whole, and *telos*, meaning goal. The prayer, then, is for God to cleanse and set us apart for divine service in such a way that everything about us will serve the goal that God has both for us personally and for the church. But since this Scripture says this is God's doing, should we assume that we have no responsibility? The answer is No. According to Romans 12:1-2, we as believers are called to do something, namely "to present your bodies as a living sacrifice." On the basis of both of these important passages from Paul, we come to the following conclusion. When I, as a believer, place my all on the altar as a living sacrifice to be used for God's mission in the world, then it is that he can integrate and orchestrate everything in my life around the purpose that he has both for me personally and for the church.

Warner, as a non-Methodist greatly influenced by holiness teaching, became convinced, in the course of time, that Scripture teaches that an inherent connection exists between entire sanctification/perfect love and the love of other believers/Christian unity. This is most clearly seen in his song "The Bond of Perfectness":

> How sweet this bond of perfectness,
>   The wondrous love of Jesus!
> A pure foretaste of heaven's bliss,
>   O fellowship so precious!
>
> O praise the Lord for love divine
>   That binds us all together!
> A thousand cords our hearts entwine
>   Forever and forever.
>
> "God over all and in us all,"
>   Thru sister and thru brother,
> No pow'r of earth or hell, withal,
>   Can rend us from each other.
>
> O mystery of heaven's peace!
>   O bond of heaven's union!
> Our souls in fellowship embrace,
>   And live in sweet communion.[5]

The refrain rejoices in "how this perfect love / Unites us all in Jesus! / One heart, and soul, and mind: we prove / The union heaven gave us."

In the current environment where relationships often are secondary to our love for things, money, and personal pleasure, the church has all the more responsibility to demonstrate other values. It is not easy for us as the church to be qualitatively different from the world around us, and, sad as it is to say, too often we are not. We have the same set of values that the world in general has. The world in general is casual about the severing of relationships when

---

5. D. S. Warner, "The Bond of Perfectness," *Worship the Lord: Hymnal of the Church of God* (Anderson, IN: Warner Press, 1989), no. 330.

they prove to be difficult, and too often so are we. But the standard set forth in the Scriptures about perfected love is that God's will is for us to be devoted both to God and to each other over the long haul, through thick and thin, and regardless of the stress and strain that we encounter. As Warner puts it: "No pow'r on earth or hell, withal, Can rend us from each other"; nor, we should add, from God. Even though such perfected love is a radical reversal of the value system of the world, nevertheless, the kind of church that, according to Scripture, pleases God has this kind of love.

A "We Reach Our Hands in Fellowship" Church

Fifth, the church that is pleasing to God is one where "we reach our hands in fellowship to every blood-washed one." It is a church that thinks of itself as an expression of God's universal church.

One finds two very different views among churches as to what the universal church is. One is that the universal church is the sum total of all local congregations. By adding up all local congregations, one arrives at the sum called the universal church. The other way is in accordance with Paul's view. Instead of beginning with local churches and ending with the universal church, he begins at the opposite point. He starts with the universal church, which is none other than the body of Christ, and understands local churches as being expressions of the one body of Christ. First Corinthians 12:12-13: "For just as the body is one and has many members, and all the members of the body, though many, are one body, so it is with Christ. For in the one Spirit we were all baptized into one body—Jews or Greeks, slaves or free—and we were all made to drink of one Spirit."

In this passage Paul sets forth the truth that we as individual believers are baptized into the universal body of Christ, not into a local congregation. It is from this perspective also that he understands local churches—they are manifestations of the one body of Christ into which all of us were baptized. In harmony with this line of thinking, then, each local church understands itself rightly only to the extent that it understands itself as a manifestation of the universal body of Christ. Every believer, as a member of the one universal church, is potentially a participant in full standing in every local congregation.

This, of course, has far-reaching implications for understanding Christian unity—an implication that D. S. Warner did not miss. It is this: when we are joined to Christ by faith we are thereby joined to all of Christ's people, irrespective of whether we particularly like them. A big part of being a Christian, then, is a matter of "getting used to the family of God." The family of God is made up of all sorts of people from many nations, cultures, racial groups, and social standings, and our job is to "get used to them."

All of this is biblical truth in which we rejoice. The challenge comes when we earnestly endeavor to put it into practice. I believe that we have a fourfold responsibility in this matter.

- It is to keep the New Testament teaching about what it means to be Christian, indeed, to be God's church, in the forefront of our teaching and preaching.

- It is to maintain a continual evaluation as to how well we are doing at being the universal church in each and every locality. How well are we communicating in the public arena that all members of the universal church will find hospitality and nourishment in each and every local congregation?

- It is to take the initiative to be in a mutually enriching relationship with all others of "like precious faith" (2 Peter 1:1 KJV); and

- It is to do all we can to demonstrate to the world our unity in Christ (see John 17).

The first in the above list is crucial. What does it mean to be Christian, indeed, to be God's church? It means that we are committed to being the circle of Christ's disciples (see Matthew 28:19-20). Furthermore, it means that we are the fellowship of those who both believe in the atoning death and resurrection of Jesus Christ, and live dead to sin and alive to Christ (see Romans 6). This, then, is the basis for everything else we say about the church.

In the course of time, however, the church had to identify itself in opposition to heresies. In doing so it fleshed out its understanding of Scripture about Jesus' relationship to the heavenly Father and to the Holy Spirit. The conclusion of the historic church is that Scripture teaches that God is a Trinity: Father, Son, and Holy Spirit. In addition, the church was called on to confess its understanding that Scripture teaches the full humanity and the full divinity of Jesus Christ.

To summarize: to be the church of biblical and historic faith is to be a fellowship of Christ's disciples who believe in his atoning death and resurrection, live dead to sin and alive to Christ, trust in the Trinitarian God of Scripture, and confess Jesus Christ as Lord, fully human and fully divine. All who are in this fellowship of Christ, then, are in the church; they are the body of Christ. Furthermore, each and every one of them, none excluded, is to be welcomed into the full fellowship of each and every local congregation of God's church and nurtured in the faith. To the degree that we take seriously the fact that we are all part and parcel of each other in the body of Christ, to that extent we will be earnest about extending hands of hospitality to brothers and sisters in other traditions of the one church. To that same degree we will, when workable, link up with them for Christian witness and service.

The *early* nineteenth-century movement led by Thomas and Alexander Campbell and Barton W. Stone had a passion for the church to live out its unity in Christ. Known as the *Restoration* Movement, it was convinced that the way for this to happen was for Christians to restore New Testament patterns in the operation of their churches, and to believe only what the Bible teaches. The *late* nineteenth-century movement led by D. S. Warner went beyond the restorationist concern. Both movements believed that the church must live out its unity in Christ to be pleasing to God, but the *Reformation* Movement led by Warner taught that the only way to that unity is the cleansing of the heart. Only when the hearts of Christians are purified of carnality will the experience of Christian unity be a reality. Whereas the emphasis in the early nineteenth-century *Restoration* Movement was on the biblical reordering of church life, the emphasis in the late nineteenth-century *Reformation* Movement was on the Holy Spirit's purification of the believer's heart. The church that is pleasing to God has its heart purified of the spirit of divisiveness.

POSSIBILITY 6

A "Kingdom of Peace" Church

Sixth, the church that is pleasing to God is a "kingdom of Peace" church. It is a church where the reign and rule of God are uppermost. According to Luke 9:1-2, "Jesus called the twelve together and gave them power and authority over all demons and to cure diseases, and he sent them out to proclaim the kingdom of God and to heal." According to verse 6, "they departed and went through the villages, bringing the good news and curing diseases everywhere."

The sixteenth-century Anabaptist movement was convinced that the kingdom was God's gift to the church here and now. They thought of the kingdom more in terms of external social structures and modes of life, while the nineteenth-century Holiness movement thought more in terms of the inner spiritual life. For this reason, the Church of God preached and taught that the kingdom of God was established in Christ, is presently experienced as Christ rules in the heart, and will be brought to consummation at the return of Christ when we shall begin enjoying heaven eternally. Both the Anabaptists and the Church of God Reformation were convinced that God calls the church to be the community of the kingdom, herald of the kingdom, and sign of the kingdom. The conviction is that the church's central message is the reality of the kingdom in the person of Jesus the Christ. But not only is the church to herald the message of the kingdom; the quality of its life should be a sign to the world that the kingdom has in fact broken into human history. The Church of God Reformation was from the beginning convinced that it is the will of God for the peacefulness of the church's reconciled relationships to be augmented by miracles of healing and restoration. These are dramatic signs of the message that the kingdom community heralds.

Whenever a church heralds something besides the good news of the kingdom, it displeases God. Whenever a church is fraught by animosity, hatred, division, or a party spirit, it displeases God. Whenever a church is devoid of miracles of healing and restoration, it displeases God. The church that pleases God is a continuation of the work assigned to the original disciples, namely, to have "power and authority over all demons and to cure diseases" and "to proclaim the kingdom of God and to heal." It is to go forth "bringing the good news and curing diseases everywhere."

A "Together We Go to Make Disciples" Church

Seventh, the church that pleases God is one that demonstrates the truth that "together we go to make disciples." It is a church that is committed both to being disciples and to making them. Matthew 28:19-20 sets forth the church's marching orders: "Go therefore and make disciples of all nations, baptizing them in the name of the Father and of the Son and of the Holy Spirit, and teaching them to obey everything that I have commanded you."

The church's mission statement does not emerge out of our business meetings. It is not the product of the church but our Lord's mandate to the church. We have no say in the matter; we either accept the divinely given mission or reject it.

The mission is to go, make disciples. A disciple of Jesus is a learner at his feet. We never get beyond our need to be in a learning relationship with him. But we do need to move on to something in addition to—not in place of—being disciples, and that is to become disciple-makers. This passage spells out how disciples are to go about making disciples. We do it first of all by "baptizing them in the name of the Father and of the Son and of the Holy Spirit." This certainly refers to water baptism, but it refers to more than that. It refers to people being inducted into the very life of the triune God. The issue, for us then, is whether we are introducing people into the very life of God. Are we helping people to get bathed in God?

The second component of making disciples is that of teaching them how to live as Jesus wants us to live, "teaching them to obey everything that I have commanded you." We never finish learning all that we need to know about living the Christlike life. At every stage of our walk with the Lord we have new lessons to learn about what it means to be his followers in the changing circumstances of life.

It is interesting that the sixteenth-century reformers mistakenly thought that the missionary mandate had already been fulfilled in the first century when the apostles went, according to tradition, to other countries. It took the seventeenth and eighteenth-century German Pietists to rediscover for Protestants that this mandate is for the church in every age. Also, in nineteenth-century America the major Protestant denominations took the missionary mandate seriously. And, from its inception, the Church of God has taken it seriously as well. We understand that the church ceases being true to itself when it forsakes the missionary mandate. In the 1950s the church commissioned the writing of a convention theme song. The result was Frederick G. Shackleton's "Together We Go to Make Disciples." Shackleton enunciates both the worldwide and the near-at-home responsibility that we have

Together we go to make disciples
for Jesus our Lord in ev'ry land;
We're reaching the lost for Christ, the Savior,
On faraway shores and near at hand.
Together we go to tell our neighbors
The message of Christ, our truest Friend.
All power is His, pow'r in earth and heaven,
And He will be with us to the end.[6]

The Church of God stands at the crossroads with this rich heritage. We must be able to enunciate it in such a way that others will be able to appreciate and embrace it. God calls us to be an evangelical church, a Bible church, a born again church, a

6. Frederick Shackleton, "Together We Go to Make Disciples," *Worship the Lord: Hymnal of the Church of God* (Anderson, IN: Warner Press, 1989), no. 297.

holiness church, a unity church, a kingdom church, and a missionary church. We sing about being this kind of church, and that is very good, indeed. By all means let us keep singing about it! But singing is not sufficient. What pleases God is that we preach and teach it, that we live it out, and that we actually function as an evangelical, Bible, born again, holiness, unity, kingdom, missionary church.

Section Four:
Guidelines at the Crossroads

GUIDELINE 1: MOVE TO "MAIN STREET"

GUIDELINE 2: ORGANIZE FOR PRAYER

GUIDELINE 3: PLAN FOR GROWTH IN CHRIST

GUIDELINE 4: ASSEMBLE TO HEAR AND
                     CELEBRATE THE WORD

GUIDELINE 5: STRATEGIZE TO WIN THE LOST

GUIDELINE 6: EXPECT THE UNEXPECTED

GUIDELINE 7: LEARN NEW WAYS TO CONFESS THE FAITH

GUIDELINE 1

Move to "Main Street"

As the Church of God comes to terms with its life at the cross-roads, certain guidelines are needed.

First, it needs to move to "Main Street." I use the term "Main Street" to indicate the center of activity of a community. In an earlier period the older denominations in the United States built their church buildings downtown. In almost any American city, town, or village, one will find church buildings that belonged to church groups like the Methodists, Presbyterians, Episcopalians, Congregationalists, Baptists, Reformed, and Catholics. They built there because the action was there. They wanted to be at the center of the community's life. But the Main Streets of many of our towns and cities are now made obsolete by shopping malls and these grand old buildings are in many cases white elephants to which dwindling congregations hang on for dear life. It is sad that these expensive, often architecturally inspiring, structures on the old Main Streets have inhibited their congregations from moving into the new Main Streets of the community. These congregations got it right in the past, but in too many cases they are inhibited from getting it right at the present time. The point is that the church, in whatever era it finds itself, needs to be located in the center of human activity whether it is the activity of rich or poor people, "red, yellow, black, or white" people, nonviolent or violent people. Church buildings are not to be places of retreat from the center of human activity; they are to be gospel places at the center of human activity. In addition, we are called to be more than enclaves of our particular brand of Christianity. If the church is nothing more than this, then any cul-de-sac will do as a location. It will do because all we are interested in is that our brand of Christians has a place to meet and enjoy our brand of Christianity. This kind of church is not interested in engagement with the community; it merely wants a place in the community to do its own thing—sing its own songs, meet its own kind, enjoy its own way of doing things, and tell its own stories to each other—this and nothing more.

Too often Church of God buildings have been built at the edge of town on a piece of donated land that some sincere soul gave with the best of intentions but without any understanding of the importance of being on Main Street. In some cases our buildings are not easily accessible, but even when they are, some do not extend a warm hand of hospitality to people in general. Some are simply Church of God clubhouses that are, for all practical purposes, off limits to people in general.

I have noticed over the years that as I check the Yellow Pages in phone directories and church pages in newspapers around the country that we are usually absent. Why is that the case? I think it grows out of a mentality that tends to be reclusive. We assume that people in general who are looking for a church simply would not be interested in considering us. In that sense, we still have not moved to Main Street. This mentality is also exhibited in the way we plan our services. I often say to our students here at Anderson University School of Theology that they should always prepare for a service on the assumption that both the most prominent people of the community and the most marginalized people will be there. Never assume that only the faithful few will be present. Always prepare on the assumption that strangers will be present. When the local church is of such quality that it is ready for all who come, the word gets out. When visitors do come they are made to feel like cherished guests, not intruders.

I know of Churches of God in the same town that function in very different ways: some function as enclaves of Church of God folks who love their traditions and shared history, and genuinely enjoy being together. They think of themselves as friendly because, indeed, they are friendly to each other. While they are not rude, outsiders soon get the message that they really do not belong simply because they do not have the shared history. Congregations like this have not yet moved to Main Street.

Others, however, think of themselves as being on Main Street and, therefore, are open to people as people. The result is that both community leaders and all kinds of needy people relate to them. The way such congregations function does not tell strangers that they are outsiders. Instead, strangers are incorporated into congregational life without having to apologize for being new to the church's traditions.

Moving to Main Street is a matter not only for local congregations but also for state, provincial, and national church life. Some states have their offices on campgrounds out in the country, away from Main Street. The Gospel Trumpet Company moved from small town to small town in the early years, always away from Main Street. When the company moved to Anderson, Indiana, it located on the east side of the White River, away from the town's Main Street and some thirty-five miles away from Main Street Indianapolis. In the course of time, the national offices have to some small degree had Main Street come to them, but they have never overtly moved to Main Street. I believe the early nineteenth-century Restoration Movement (Churches of Christ, Christian Churches, Disciples of Christ) is so much larger and more influential in cultural and religious life than the late nineteenth-century Reformation Movement because the Restoration Movement moved to Main Street early on.

At every level of church life, it is time to move to Main Street. The reason for doing so is not so that we can be bigger and more influential but to follow the example of our Lord, who is head of the church. Jesus, in his incarnational ministry, made the Temple in Jerusalem the center of his ministry. He taught and healed at the center of political, cultural, and religious life. It was at Jerusalem that he was tried, crucified, and raised from the dead. It was in Jerusalem that the Holy Spirit was poured out on the day of Pentecost. And as the empowered church went forth with the gospel, it targeted the synagogues in cities around the

Mediterranean world. God and God's church reached people by going to Main Street.

Yes, Jesus sometimes went apart from the crowds. Yes, both he and the church had ministries in out-of-the-way places. However, these occasional retreats were always related to the center of strategic activity on Main Street.

Organize for Prayer

The second guideline for us at the crossroads is that we organize for prayer. The church in the New Testament was a church of prayer.

They planned to pray and they prayed to plan. One of the most remarkable stories in Christian history is the hundred-year prayer meeting of the Moravian Church. On August 27, 1727, twenty-four male and twenty-four female Moravian Christians agreed to spend one in every twenty-four hours in intercessory prayer. Within a short while, the wider membership entered into this practice, called the "Hourly Intercession," which continued for over a hundred years. John Wesley was greatly influenced by the praying Moravians. It was in one of their Bible study meetings that in 1738 he felt his heart strangely warmed, leading to the great Wesleyan revival that jumped the Atlantic and spawned both the Holiness Movement and later the Church of God reformation movement. Great missionary outreach, spiritual revival, and social witness paralleled this period of concerted prayer.

Something good happens to the church when it plans to pray together and actually carries through with it. When Ed Nelson was pastor of my home church, Park Place in Anderson, he announced that every Wednesday night, along with all the other options offered, he would be conducting a session of prayer. It would not be used to talk about prayer, nor about requests; it would be for prayer itself. I remember one night when another man of the congregation prayed. I have known him for almost forty years and have been in the same church with him for over twenty years, yet we had never been in a setting where each of us prayed extemporaneously. Probably he had heard me offer the main prayer in a corporate service of worship, but never in an informal setting, and I had never heard him pray. I had always known him to be a faithful Christian. We always greeted each other in a hospitable way, but that was it. Something happened, though, in that prayer meeting when each of us poured out our hearts in earnest prayer. He became more to me than just another faithful member of the church. I was allowed to peer into his heart that night, and he into mine. As a result, our relationship changed. When we saw each other, it was much more than a matter of general hospitality. When I was absent from church due to other responsibilities, he noticed, and when I returned he'd ask where I had been. Our conversations included more than a polite hello to each other; they included animated sharing about the stuff of life. Being at prayer meeting together changed our relationship.

A church that prays together is a transformed church. But it does not just happen; we have to be intentional about it.

GUIDELINE 3

Plan for Growth in Christ

The third guideline for us at the crossroads is that we plan for growth in Christ. To be people who "accept Christ as their personal Savior" is not a sufficient goal for church life. That is basic, but it is only the beginning. The goal is that persons mature in Christ. Again, this does not just happen; we have to plan for it.

John Wesley was intentional about people maturing in Christ. In Wesley's *A Plain Account of Christian Perfection*, he quotes, with approval, one of his followers who says: "That part of our economy [that is, our way of doing things], the private weekly meetings for prayer, examination, and particular exhor[t]ation (sic), has been the greatest means of deepening and confirming every blessing that was received by the word preached, and of diffusing it to others, who could not attend the public ministry, whereas, without this religious connection and intercourse, the most ardent attempts, by mere preaching, have proved of no lasting use."

The pastoral question of early Methodist preachers was, "How is it with your soul?" That is the most important question we in the church can learn to ask each other in the twenty-first century. We need to learn how to deal with the need for people to mature in Christ. In too many cases we are satisfied with warm bodies being in church and not sufficiently concerned about their maturity in Christ. But it does not happen automatically. It happens when the church intends for it to happen. The way we go about being the church should be determined by our agenda for enhancing people's spiritual health. This health includes the health of both the church in general and of individuals as well—each and every single one of them whether old or young or in between, whether male or female, whether newcomer or long-timer, whether troublemaker, compliant, or cooperative. How is it with their souls? And how is it with the church's soul?

GUIDELINE 4

Assemble to Hear and to Celebrate the Word

The fourth guideline at the crossroads is that we assemble to hear and to celebrate the Word. The reformation and renewal of the church that took place in the sixteenth century was Word-centered. Corporate worship became services of the Word. Preaching was revived. People went to church to be instructed about the teachings of the Bible and more particularly about the gospel. As much as ever—and perhaps even more than ever—people are looking for meaning and purpose for their lives.

J. Gordon Melton and Robert L. Moore, in their book *The Cult Experience: Responding to the New Religious Pluralism*, hold that one of the reasons some persons join cult groups is because both the church and the university leave them in a conceptual vacuum. Consequently, they find it difficult to make "sense out of the confusion of their existence."[1] And so, needing a conceptual frame for understanding life, they turn to cult groups that claim to have the answers. Cults put the jigsaw puzzle of life together. But the church, in too many instances, has become lackadaisical about the content of the faith. Too often preaching and teaching do not help to put the jigsaw puzzle of life together; instead they add to the confusion.

Darlene and I found ourselves in downtown Cleveland, Ohio, on a Sunday morning and, as is our custom, we went to church.

---

1. J. Gordon Melton and Robert L. Moore, *The Cult Experience: Responding to the New Religious Pluralism* (New York: Pilgrim Press, 1982), 34.

The nearest to our hotel was Old Stone Presbyterian Church. As we approached the steps of the church, a city worker, who was on a job in front of the building, called out to us, "Does that church have a good preacher?" I told him that I did not know since I was a visitor. But the question he asked is similar to the one many people ask these days about the church itself: "Does it have anything worthwhile to say and does it know how to say it? Is the church itself a good preacher?"

Impressive programs keep people coming until they get tired of the programs. It is only when people are well-nurtured regularly from the Word that a spiritual robustness develops. When the church gathers, it needs to do so both to hear the Word and to celebrate its transforming power at work in people's lives.

Strategize to Win the Lost

The fifth guideline at the crossroads is to strategize to win the lost. The Sunday school movement beginning in the eighteenth century, the vigorous expansion of the missionary movement in the eighteenth and nineteenth, and the great revivals during the same centuries, both in Great Britain and in North America, were great movements of the Holy Spirit. But they were also movements driven by people who strategized to win the lost.

With the population of the world growing at an astounding rate, the church's mission takes on new urgency. If we are still convinced that Jesus is the Way, the Truth, and the Life, our job is becoming incrementally tougher. In order to penetrate the burgeoning world that knows not the joy of Christ, we need to strategize more carefully and effectively than ever. It will not happen merely by hoping that it happens, or even by praying that it happens. Hoping and praying have to be linked with the church's strategizing for it to happen. Just as the church in the first century had a strategy so must the church in the twenty-first century.

How shall we win the lost who attend the services of our local congregations? Are we satisfied with the presence of their warm bodies, or are we dissatisfied with leaving it at that? Are we effective in our outreach to those who attend our services Sunday after Sunday? Are we content simply that they are churchgoers? And how does a local congregation go about winning the lost just outside the doors of its building? When we begin taking seriously these questions, that is the best first step toward effective participation with the wider church community for more expansive strategies elsewhere. Winning the lost "way off somewhere else" can easily become an inoculation against attempting to win the lost inside and just outside our own doors. As one person has put it: "I am not interested in how many more people attend your services this year than last year. I am interested in how many more disciples there are."

GUIDELINE 6

Expect the Unexpected

The sixth guideline at the crossroads is to expect the unexpected. A common characteristic of revivals through the centuries has been the element of divine surprise. The same was true of the camp meetings of the nineteenth century, and of Pentecostalism beginning in the early twentieth century. It is true of the Charismatic movement that began during the mid-twentieth century. More recently we see it in such movements as Promise Keepers. Whatever one's assessment of these movements, they remind us that the Spirit is not preprogrammed to function according to our plans. The Spirit does have boundaries: those boundaries are in the shape of Jesus the Christ as revealed in Scripture. According to Scripture, the Holy Spirit always works in accordance with what has been revealed in Christ. Christ, then, is always the measure by which we can discern whether something is truly of the Spirit. The Spirit always works in conformity with Christ, but his work inevitably breaks the clay jars of our humanly developed religious life, and that is often unsettling.

People of the twenty-first century will not tolerate boredom. For one thing, they have too many options at their fingertips, and they are too mobile to subject themselves to the boredom of human religiosity. Life is too short to dedicate oneself to religious boredom when Holy Spirit-inspired excitement is on the next block. Furthermore, the excitement of the Spirit is too much a part of general knowledge for any church to keep it a secret from its people for long. It is no secret to anyone who is halfway tuned into the Christian world. In the course of time, those who are incarcerated in prisons of holy drudgery will begin wondering why they should miss out on the holy fun. And so, when they finally awaken to the fact that the prison doors are open, it is likely that they will escape.

For a church to be truly open to the Spirit, it must be willing to expect the unexpected whenever it gathers for worship. As John 3:8 teaches, just as "the wind blows where it chooses," so does the Holy Spirit. We simply cannot manage the Spirit. Therefore, unless we want to run the risk of working against the Spirit, we had better become flexible to the Spirit.

Again I say, this is not a plea for anything goes. Nor is it a plea that we allow anything and everything that claims to be of the Spirit. Something is of the Spirit not because someone says it is; it is of the Spirit only when it passes the tests of Christ and Scripture. When it passes these tests we can have the confidence that it truly is the work of the Holy Spirit; all other phenomena are either of human origin or worse. But this one and only Christ-shaped, Scripture-described Spirit is the Spirit who converts, transforms, heals, blesses, fills, guides, calls, sends forth, and so much more. No church will make it far into the twenty-first century unless it expects the unexpected brought about by the Christ-shaped, Scripture-described Holy Spirit.

GUIDELINE 7

Learn New Ways to Confess the Faith

The seventh guideline is that as a church we need to find additional ways to confess our Christian faith. "What do you people believe?" is a question we are often asked. It is a fair question and deserves an answer. Here is one possibility:

A Confession of Christian Faith According to Scripture

God and Salvation
We believe in the triune God: Father, Son, and Holy Spirit (see Matthew 28:19).

Along with the ancient people of Israel, we confess that "the Lord is our God, the Lord alone. You shall love the Lord your God with all your heart, and with all your soul, and with all your might" (Deuteronomy 6:4-5).

In agreement with the New Testament church, we confess that "Jesus is Lord" (1 Corinthians 12:3).

In the words of the ancient church, we confess "that Christ died for our sins in accordance with the scriptures, and that he was buried, and that he was raised on the third day" (1 Corinthians 15:3-4).

In harmony with a New Testament hymn of faith, we confess that Jesus Christ "is the image of the invisible God, the firstborn of all creation; for in him all things in heaven and on earth were created, things visible and invisible, whether thrones or dominions or rulers or powers—all things have been created through him and for him. He himself is before all things, and in him all things hold together. He is the head of the body, the church; he is the beginning, the firstborn from the dead, so that he might come to have first place in everything. For in him all the fullness of God was pleased to dwell, and through him God was pleased to reconcile to himself all things, whether on earth or in heaven, by making peace through the blood of his cross" (Colossians 1:15-20).

We have been buried with Christ "by baptism into death, so that, just as Christ was raised from the dead by the glory of the Father, so we too might walk in newness of life" (Romans 6:4).

We rejoice at the outpouring of the Holy Spirit on the day of Pentecost, and experience the fulfillment of Jesus' promise when he said that "the Advocate, the Holy Spirit, whom the Father will send in my name, will teach you everything, and remind you of all that I have said to you" (John 14:26).

We hearken to Paul's admonition to "be filled with the Spirit" (Ephesians 5:18), and "to lead a life worthy of the calling to which you have been called, with all humility and gentleness, with patience, bearing with one another in love, making every effort to maintain the unity of the Spirit in the bond of peace" (Ephesians 4:1-3).

We know that as believers we are instructed to present our "bodies as a living sacrifice, holy and acceptable to God, which is "spiritual worship" (Romans 12:1). And we trust in the fulfillment of the benediction: "May the God of peace himself sanctify you entirely; and may your spirit and soul and body be kept sound and blameless at the coming of our Lord Jesus Christ. The one who calls you is faithful, and he will do this" (1 Thessalonians 5:23-24).

The Church and Unity

We affirm in the words of Scripture that "there is one body and one Spirit, just as you were called to the one hope of your calling, one Lord, one faith, one baptism, one God and Father of all, who is above all and through all and in all. But each of us was given grace according to the measure of Christ's gift" (Ephesians 4:4-7).

In accordance with the guidelines of Scripture, we take delight in the fellowship of God's church, "not neglecting to meet together, as is the habit of some, but encouraging one another, and all the more as [we] see the Day approaching" (Hebrews 10:25).

We enjoy singing "psalms and hymns and spiritual songs ... making melody to the Lord in [our] hearts" (Ephesians 5:19).

We are committed to the ministry of anointing "with oil in the name of the Lord," and we believe that "the prayer of faith will save the sick, and the Lord will raise them up; and anyone who has committed sins will be forgiven" (James 5: 14-15).

We commune at table where our Lord, with broken loaf, says, "This is my body that is for you. Do this in remembrance of me," and, with chalice uplifted, says, "This cup is the new covenant in my blood" (1 Corinthians 11:24, 25).

We wash each other's feet even as Jesus himself washes our feet to cleanse and renew us for the pilgrim journey of faith (see John 13:1-20).

We are nourished by "the sacred writings that are able to instruct [us] for salvation through faith in Christ Jesus." We believe that "all scripture is inspired by God and is useful for teaching, for reproof, for correction, and for training in righteousness, so that everyone who belongs to God may be proficient, equipped for every good work" (2 Timothy 3:15, 16–17).

We seek to be part of the answer to our Lord's prayer "that they may all be one. As you, Father, are in me and I am in you, may they also be in us, so that the world may believe that you have sent me" (John 17:21).

We anticipate the time when the church will live out the reality we have in Christ that "there is no longer Jew or Greek, there is no longer slave or free, there is no longer male and female; for all of you are one in Christ Jesus" (Galatians 3:28).

Mission and Hope

With gladness, we accept the commission of Jesus to "make disciples of all nations, baptizing them in the name of the Father and of the Son and of the Holy Spirit, and teaching them to obey everything that I have commanded you" (Matthew 28:19-20).

We desire, as people of the kingdom, to minister in the name of Christ who, in the words of Isaiah, said, "The Spirit of the Lord is upon me, because he has anointed me to bring good news to the poor. He has sent me to proclaim release to the captives and recovery of sight to the blind, to let the oppressed go free, to proclaim the year of the Lord's favor" (Luke 4:18-19).

We are committed to the gospel of the kingdom, which is "righteousness and peace and joy in the Holy Spirit" (Romans 14:17).

In faith, hope, and love, we look forward to that time when "the Lord himself, with a cry of command, with the archangel's call and with the sound of God's trumpet, will descend from heaven, and the dead in Christ will rise first. Then we who are alive, who are left, will be caught up in the clouds together with them to meet the Lord in the air; and so we will be with the Lord forever" (1 Thessalonians 4:16-17).

Maranatha! "Come, Lord Jesus!" (Revelation 22:20).

Section Five:
Concluding Statements

I conclude with the following hopes regarding the Church of God. **I hope that we will as a church enter into conversations with the broader church.** Conversations are taking place around the world between widely divergent Christian traditions for the purpose of mutual understanding and enrichment, not for the purpose of merging their respective church organizations. Some of the formal theological conversations taking place are between Southern Baptists and Roman Catholics, between Reformed churches and Pentecostals, between Pentecostal and Holiness groups, between Churches of Christ, Independent Christian Churches and the Disciples of Christ. The whole list is too long to include here, but as of this writing we are not on it.

Such conversations have at least three benefits.

- They provide the opportunity to share our insights with others of "like precious faith."

- They provide the opportunity to be enriched by others of "like precious faith."

- And such conversations provide the only setting in which our own theological understandings can be developed as carefully as they ought to be. As long as we are simply talking to ourselves, we do not have to be bothered by the questions and issues raised by outsiders to our tradition. The result is that we tend to become lazy theologically and sloppy in our thinking.

I hope that we will attend to the issue of ministerial formation. Unless we decide what kind of ministers we want to have, we will perish as a church fellowship. In too many instances our ordained ministers do not have biblical, theological, historical, practical, ethical, moral, and spiritual preparation for the work of the ordained ministry. (Thank God for the many, many exceptions!) But we are too haphazard about the whole process of the spiritual, theological, and professional formation of ministers. We are paying a very high price for this lackadaisical approach. God is not pleased and neither should we be with the disorder that this brings. The people of God deserve better.

The wider church has much to teach us in this regard. Since we began as a come-out group that for the most part cut itself off from the wider church and rejected it as Babylon, our tendency is to invent everything brand new. We have to learn our lessons the long, painful way by making many unnecessary mistakes. As I often said to our children when they were still at home, "You can be educated in one of two universities of life. Either you can choose the University of Collected Wisdom or the University of Hard Knocks." The same is true of young church groups such as our own. We can choose either to learn in the University of Collected Wisdom of the Wider Church, or we will inevitably find ourselves in the University of Hard Knocks where we learn by trial and error. Regardless of whether a church finds itself in the first university or the second, it will always have plenty of tests, failures, and challenges. The failures will be fewer in the University of Collected Wisdom. Up to this point we do not have a carefully stated theology of Christian ministry; consequently, we tend to be lax when it comes to ordination processes.

Too often ordination tends to be little more than our recognition of someone's desire to be recognized as an ordained minister. That is not good enough. We have ordained ministers who never preach, and/or teach, or lead in worship. We have ordained ministers who have no preparation in Bible, theology, history, and the practice of ministry beyond what most people in local congregations have. We have ordained ministers who are simply leaders in the local church. We have ordained ministers who are ordained primarily because they are in a ministerial family.

In much of the wider church, ordination is to the "ministry of Word and Sacrament." Though that terminology may sound strange to us, it means that persons are ordained for the express purpose of preaching and/or teaching the Word and leading in worship. They are ordained not because they are more spiritual than others are. They are ordained not simply because they have a job with a salary from a church organization. They are ordained not because they are in a ministerial family. They are ordained not because they simply want this status for tax purposes or standing in the church. They are ordained because they are prepared in ways that others in the church are not in their understanding of Scripture, theology, history, and the practice of ministry.

They are ordained because they have a special ministerial formation that prepares them to minister in that particular church tradition. They are ordained because they are able to preach and/or teach the Word and are able to lead people in the worship of God. The reference to leading in worship is not about musical skills; it is about the ability to lead the people of God in prayer, in devotional expressions, in the Lord's Supper, and in corporate worship. In much of the wider church, the ordained ministry is not for persons who hold staff jobs in religious organizations; rather, it is for persons who are called and prepared to preach and/or teach the Word, and lead the people of God in worship.

I hope that we will define what it means for a congregation to be listed in the *Yearbook of the Church of God.* As things now stand, the only thing that one can count on is that every congregation listed is registered by a state, provincial, or district assembly. Being listed does not necessarily mean that a congregation supports state or national work; it does not necessarily mean that traditional Church of God understandings are preached and taught; it does not necessarily mean that the congregation even thinks of itself as being associated with the Church of God. Why, then, are these particular congregations listed together? Certainly they are not the only congregations in the United States and Canada that are preaching the gospel. What sets these particular congregations apart so that it is appropriate to list them in a special book?

I hope that we will live out our historic message of holiness and unity. My sense is that having gotten to the other side of legalism, we have given up on trying to define what holiness of life looks like. In some congregations—and in the personal lives of some—an anything-goes approach is taken. Another problem is that meanspiritedness, segregationist policies, and church splits have been allowed in too many instances to go unchecked. Too often we make easy peace with such negative witnesses to a unity message. One of the reasons we quit using "A united church for a divided world" as a slogan for our CBH radio broadcast was that, in some cases, it was publicly embarrassing because churches in local listening areas had been through splits, were segregationists, and were mean spirited. These local anomalies discredited the slogan, and made us look like fools.

Part of the culture of being Church of God should be the seriousness with which we take the message of personal holiness and Christian unity so that local communities find the integrity of our message lived out among them. We, of all people, should have congregations that are known in their respective localities as fellowships where people practice the skills of conflict resolution. All of our churches should be known as centers of reconciliation. Our churches always ought to be sites for interracial life and mission. Our churches should always be the exceptions to the rule in segregationist cultures. Church splits should be unheard of among us.

To be sure, the kind of thing I am talking about is hard stuff, but grand and glorious truths get through to others only when the local congregational life is exceptionally devoted to the hard stuff of living out those truths. In an earlier era, H. M. Riggle used a strange-sounding term when he said that the church is to be a gazing-stock fellowship.[1] By that he meant that the church should be a gathering of Spirit-empowered people who so attract the world's attention that they gaze at us and glorify God.

I hope that first and foremost we will be kingdom people, lovers of truth, and doers of justice, and not allow ourselves to be defined by any political, cultural, or religious agenda. Political

---

1. H. M. Riggle, "Do We Need a Creed Apart from the Bible?" *The Gospel Trumpet*, May 21, 1925, 2.

parties, cultural movements, or religious affiliations should never set our agenda as a church fellowship. We will not be completely at home anywhere. No organization, movement, or affiliation can ever count on us to be one hundred percent in their court. With our ultimate goal of being kingdom people who love truth and do justice, we will inevitably cross the boundaries of human organizations, cultural movements, and religious designations.

Our focus has always been on what it means to be the community of the kingdom, lovers of God's truth, and doers of justice. To the extent that this leads us into association with others of like mind, well and good, but we will never sell our souls to them. Our souls are captivated by the kingdom, by God's truth, and by God's justice.

I hope that we will develop a pastoral attitude toward all of our people. For a long time I have been troubled about how easy it is for people to come through our churches and then get lost when they either drop out or move. If we were to develop a unified approach to staying in touch with the people who either grow up in our churches or come through them, as well as staying in touch with those who are long-term members, we would be functioning in the mode of the good shepherd of Luke 15 who is not willing to make peace with the loss of even one. In far too many cases we do not do well in tracking people, passing along information from one congregation to another about those who have moved, and staying connected with persons who are going through transitional times in their lives such as college, the military, or crisis.

I hope that we will develop a sense of family connection so that wherever we find one of our churches, we will experience it as being at home. I realize that being at home has to do with many important dimensions of our Christian life. Here I am talking about being at home in the network of churches called the Church of God. This network should be so strong that wherever we find ourselves we know that we are at home there, too.

Often service clubs such as Rotarians and Optimists have more camaraderie than do some of our churches. When members of a service club attend the meetings of the same club in other places, typically they have a sense of being at home. Though they may have known no one in the local club prior to the meeting, the sense of connection is so great that when the meeting is over they know that they have been at home. The lack of such connection among some of our churches is astounding. We are not adequately nurturing this historic value among us. Increasingly we tend not to think in terms of the Church of God network of relationships.

In no way is this to downplay the sense of being connected to the broader church—those who know me well know how devoted I am to that—but it seems to me that if God still has a role for us to play as a particular fellowship, then surely we ought to have a warm, hospitable connectedness that extends beyond the local congregation to the rest of the network. Of course, there are many examples of such connectedness among us and in that I rejoice. But the general trend is in the opposite direction.

I hope that we will learn to treasure the intergenerational character of the church. One of the traditional values of small churches is their intergenerational character. Younger people hear the testimonies of older people, and vice versa. Friendships between the generations are established that in many cases last for a lifetime. Older people mentor young people; youth are taught by older people how to take leadership roles in the life of the church; and the older people are never retired from Christian service.

We face this challenge today in our larger churches as well as in district and national work. How do we go about mentoring the young? How do we continue reaping the benefits of the wisdom of age? How do we take advantage of the enrichment that the full spectrum of age, experience, energies, creativity, and wisdom provides? We need to be more intentional about this full spectrum in our local church life as well as in our district and national church life.

I hope that we will develop a consistent educational program from the earliest level of Christian education in the local church through the adult department, into college and seminary. What I mean by this is that what we teach at one level of education should not be contradictory to what we teach at another level. Obviously, what we teach, the issues dealt with, the methodology used, and the depth and breadth of the experience will be vastly different at different age levels. But what we teach to a kindergarten child in Sunday school should not have to be unlearned when he or she grows up and finds out "how things really are." I am always bothered when I hear people talking about having to discard their childhood understandings when they study at another level. What we teach about the Bible and Christian life in the Sunday school at any grade level should not have to be scrapped when the student studies at one of our colleges or at seminary. And as a professor, I never like to hear anyone at the seminary say that it is all right to say certain things here that one could never say in a local church. Furthermore, I dislike the idea that what we teach as Christian values in a local church no longer applies when one is exposed to the values espoused in our institutions of higher education.

The consistency that I am hoping for would, of course, require

- mutual respect between the various levels of Christian education,

- persistent communication between the different venues of Christian education, and

- cooperation between all components of our Christian education endeavors.

I saw this kind of consistency when I was minister of Christian education at the Hyde Park Congregational Church in Boston. The materials used in our local Christian education program were written not only by local ministers but also by the top scholars in the fields of Bible, theology, and history. Christian educators in local parishes enriched Christian educators in educational institutions, and vice versa. I was impressed with the scholarly understanding of educators in local churches and with the practical understanding of educators in colleges and seminaries. Furthermore, well-known Bible scholars, historians, and theologians were attuned to the developmental difference between graduate level Christian education and Christian education in the local church. They were able to write helpfully for local church education because they had not only scholarly preparation, but also a high view of the work of the local church, and expertise in communicating at that level. And persons in local ministry were able to write material with intellectual integrity. Consistent Christian education from kindergarten through graduate level work was an intentional goal—and a noble one it was.

I hope that we will be known far and wide by our Christian hospitality toward all people. We should treat all people as being precious in the sight of God and all believers as beloved brothers and sisters in Christ. Hospitality is both a spirit and an art. Some congregations have neither; others have one or the other; I want us to have both.

The *spirit of hospitality* is an evidence of the work of the Holy Spirit in our lives. The *art of hospitality* has to be learned.

Hospitality is much more than friendliness. Whereas friendliness is a momentary act of kindness—for instance, a handshake, the nod of the head, a pleasant greeting—hospitality is the gracious reception of another into one's life.

Persons and churches may have the spirit of hospitality but may not have many of the skills of hospitality. How does a church in its national life graciously receive the wider fellowship of Christians into its life? How does a local congregation graciously receive the stranger, the outsider, and the one who is different into the circle of its love without compromising its identity as the community of Christian faith? What distinguishes distinctively Christian hospitality from hospitality in general? These are questions I hope we will ask ourselves on a regular basis.

I hope that the time will come when the spirit of Christian hospitality identifies us both in the public arena and in the church arena. I hope that we will become especially skilled in this Christian art and practice.

~

This, then, is my understanding of who we are at this juncture in our history—our challenges, our opportunities, and our possibilities. Good things can happen at the crossroads if we

- are faithful to living out the possibilities of being the church that is pleasing to God,

- maximize our opportunities, and

- face up to our challenges.

I offer what I believe are important guidelines for our work together. As a Christian brother, I share my personal hopes.

While writing this book, I have found myself making deeper commitments to God and to both God's universal church and the Church of God. I have realized once again that in the last analysis things get changed as each does the little that each can do. I am grateful that "little is much when God is in it." To the extent that God is in the little that you and I say and do, it can become much for the sake of the kingdom.

BOOK 2

VISION
for the
CHURCH OF GOD
at the
CROSSROADS

DEDICATION

To the local congregations that have formed me spiritually, nurtured me—and later my family—in the faith, and have given me opportunities for ministry.

First Church of God in Portageville, Missouri, where my parents grew up in the faith, married, and found nurture when they gave birth to me as their first-born;

First Church of God in Dexter, Missouri, where I first remember the pleasant sounds, sights, and emotions of being in church;

First Church of God in Piggott, Arkansas, where I gained images of dramatic conversions, testimonies of faith, victorious shouting, dinners on the grounds, playing after church, business meetings, Sunday school in a damp basement, and my first introduction to a movie projector;

First Church of God in Mount Carmel, Illinois, which in many ways became my measuring rod as to what it means to be a good church, and where, in the course of time, I preached my first sermons;

Pinehurst Church of God in Birmingham, Alabama, where I declared my faith in water baptism and where I stumbled through my first public testimony given in a Wednesday night service as the congregation sanctioned every trembling word;

Park Road Church of God in Anderson, Indiana, where I moved to a new level of leadership as a teacher first of teen-agers and later of college students;

First Church of God in Greeneville, Tennessee, where for the first time I had full pastoral responsibilities for a whole summer while the senior pastor was on a trip abroad;

Sixth Avenue Church of God in Decatur, Alabama, where I learned how to work on a pastoral team serving as youth minister for two summers;

The Church of God at Malden, Massachusetts, where I experienced for the first time the full challenge of being the called pastor, participated in local community and inter-church life as pastor of a church, and took responsibility in the area work of the Church of God;

First Congregational Church of Hyde Park, in Boston, Massachusetts, where I was regularly called upon to explain my different orientation to what it means to be church, and where I learned to appreciate at a deeper level Church of God values and perspectives;

East Ashman Church of God in Midland, Michigan, which called me as their pastor and demonstrated how healthy churches are supposed to function;

Park Place Church of God in Anderson, Indiana. which nurtured me during part of my college and seminary years, and has nurtured our whole family in its loving arms since my coming to the seminary assignment in 1976.

ACKNOWLEDGEMENTS

I am grateful to the following persons who read the first draft of this book and offered many helpful suggestions. They asked questions, raised issues, and spoke words of encouragement that guided the writing of the final product, though I alone take full responsibility for all that is said here.

Thanks to my seminary colleagues Dean David L. Sebastian, Dr. Juanita Leonard, and Dr. James W. Lewis—all three of whom are active participants in the wide spectrum of our church life; to Dr. Arlo F. Newell, former editor in chief of *Vital Christianity* and minister at large throughout the Church of God; to Dr. Ronald Duncan, until recently pastor in Texas, and general director of Church of God Ministries; to Rev. Jeannette Flynn and Rev. Jim Davey, leaders of the Congregational Ministries Team of Church of God Ministries; to seminarian Jim Feirtag; and to the intergenerational ministers in my family: my younger brother Pastor Rod Stafford and my father and step-mother Revs. D. C. and Arietta Shock Stafford.

INTRODUCTION

Since the publication of *Church of God at the Crossroads*, I have had the privilege of being in conversation with many persons throughout the world. Some have chosen to send comments through e-mail. Others have sent letters either to me directly or to the national office of Church of God Ministries. In some cases, I have had phone conversations or personal visits. In other instances, the feedback has been in response to the questionnaire sent out to career missionaries of the Church of God for the purpose of their consulting with leaders in their respective areas. Responses were received from South America, the Caribbean, and from Africa.

Another important piece of the conversation has been in connection with Crossroads conferences conducted in various parts of the United States, in Canada, in Asia, and in Europe. And lastly, I was very much the beneficiary of the Crossroads conferences held at the North American Convention in 2000 and in 2001. The participants in these conferences represented the ethnic, cultural, and theological diversity of the church. African-American voices were heard in almost all of the United States conferences. The Hispanic request to translate Crossroads was readily given, thus providing the opportunity for conversation within that important dimension of our church life.

My travels to Asia and meetings with church leaders there were made possible with the help of Outreach Ministries of the Church of God, the church in Japan, and the church in Hong Kong. This whole project was strongly encouraged by President James L. Edwards of Anderson University and Dean David L. Sebastian of the School of Theology. They expressed this encouragement not only in personal words, but also by granting me a sabbatical during the second semester of academic year 2000-01 and by financial support from special funds for faculty enrichment, for extensive travels in twelve European countries.

This widespread conversation has given me new perspective on our church fellowship as we face the challenges at the crossroads.

First of all, I have new appreciation for the spiritual qualities I have observed:

- **Sacrificial living.** For instance, I rejoiced at the dedication of the workers at Camp Challenge in Alaska, and the work campers from Ohio and Kentucky who dedicated themselves to all kinds of tasks and jobs, at their own expense.

- **Tenderness of spirit.** In not a single instance in this past year and a half have I experienced a meanness of spirit, even when there were major disagreements.

- **Earnestness of endeavors.** One of many examples was the work of the Asia Team—Summer Siehl and Patrick and Jamie Nachtigall—in putting together the weeklong meeting in Hong Kong for the Asian leaders to talk about issues facing the Church of God at the crossroads.

- **Conviction about who we are and about certain doctrinal matters.** In every conference I have held, the level of doctrinal conviction expressed was immeasurably higher than I had previously imagined.

- **Faithfulness to Christ, to his church, and to his truth.** I saw this especially in the intensity of church leaders in Hungary as they face enormous challenges to staying afloat as a church fellowship.

- **Dedicated service.** An example is the quality of work being done under difficult circumstances at places like the Mediterranean Bible College in Beirut, Lebanon; Bibelschule der Gemeinde Gottes in Fritzlar, Germany; and Kima International School of Theology in Kenya.

- **Patience with the process and with God's timing.** As we deal with the enormously wide-ranging changes taking place in the structured life of the Church of God, I stand amazed at the collective patience.

- **Expectancy about the future and about what God is doing and is about to do**. Why else do people keep expending significant blocks of time such as two to five days coming to Crossroads conferences, and leaving with a sense of anticipation about good things that are about to happen?

Second, I am greatly encouraged about the remarkable depth of conviction regarding the historic perspectives and values of the Church of God. The attitude I encounter time after time is that, even though we may indeed be at a crossroads, we intend not to let loose of that which we believe we have been entrusted by God to proclaim, teach, and live. The church with which I have been in contact wants to:

- Leave no doubt that it is to be identified in terms of classical Christianity regarding its belief in the one eternally triune God—Father, Son and Holy Spirit—and its belief in the full humanity and full divinity of Jesus Christ.

- State forthrightly that the Bible is our rule of faith and practice.

- Emphasize that we are to preach and teach all that

scripture affirms in light of what the Bible teaches about Jesus Christ.

- Reaffirm the themes that are important in our history to the extent they are truly biblical themes.

- Make clear that we believe in:
    □ The necessity of personal repentance and faith for salvation.
    □ Being born again.
    □ Living the holy life.
    □ Personal salvation as the way into the church.
    □ The unity of all believers.
    □ The interdependence of unity and holiness.
    □ The missionary mandate of the church.
    □ Jesus as the revelation of the kingdom; the kingdom here and now as Jesus rules as Lord of history, of the church, and in the hearts of believers; and the consummation of the kingdom at the end of the age.
    □ The one and only return of Christ at the end of the age.
    □ The security of our salvation being dependent on our remaining in Christ by faith.
    □ Living in the sanctifying power of the Holy Spirit as victors over sin.
    □ The final judgment leading to heaven or hell.
    □ Jesus Christ as the only means of salvation.

These are themes I heard repeatedly throughout the course of my conversations.

Third, I heard practical concerns enunciated regularly:

- We want better communications among ourselves. Too often, we do not know what is going on in other segments of church life.

- We need a better system of accountability rather than ignoring the rest of the church in the pursuit of independent agendas.

- We need to continue working on matters of ordination and credentialing so that we have in place procedures that are standard for all.

- We need statements about what we believe so that our implicit understandings are explicitly stated. We are not calling for anything that is legalistically enforced on the church, but for the clarification of our historic understandings of biblical faith.

- We need guidelines as to how to go about being church in relation to God, to the world, to our historic vision, to each other within our fellowship, and in relation to other Christians who are not a part of our fellowship.

With these observations about the Church of God at the crossroads, I then asked myself whether I had any further obligation. The answer is found in this book.

One of the truisms of church life is this: "Where there is no vision, the people perish" (Prov 29:18 KJV). I add two more: Where there is no reflection, the people perish. Where there is no action, the people perish. If we do not have before us the historic, biblical vision concerning who we are and what God calls us to be and do, we come unraveled as a people. If we never reflect on whether our understanding of the vision is adequate and whether we are convinced that it is still of God, and if we never reflect on how well we are living out the vision, and on what we need to correct, accelerate, or eliminate in light of the vision, we will perish from stagnancy. If we never take action on the basis of our reflection we will perish from sluggishness.

Since vision is the key word throughout the book, I offer the following definition: A vision is a defining view that identifies who we are and determines how we should then live and work.

And so the purpose of this book is to enunciate as clearly as I can the historic vision of the Church of God, to reflect on it, and to offer suggestions for action. I offer the following with gratitude for the blessed fellowship of the church that has immeasurably enriched me. I offer it in the spirit of prayer to the Lord of the church that it may in some small way strengthen the church's witness. And I offer it as an expression of love for God and his one universal church.

CHAPTER 1

Identifying the Historic Vision

The Church of God has a historic vision as to the kind of church that pleases God. The themes that have a solid biblical foundation and that are common among us all are seven in number. These are our persistent, time-tested anchors. To put it another way, they are the fabric of what it means to be God's church. The framework for this fabric will be set forth in chapters 3 and 4, and the more detailed texture of this fabric will be set forth in the "As Christians, Here We Stand" document in chapter 5. Since the 1880s we have preached these seven themes. We have published articles, books, and pamphlets about them. We have sung about them. In a book like this, the easiest way to refer to this historic vision is to use songs that celebrate the themes. I shall identify the themes, give a short descriptive statement about each, and then quote from at least two of our songs for each theme:

1. We are called to be a **gospel church**. Everything we do and say is to be permeated with the good news of God's redeeming and sanctifying grace made known to us in Jesus Christ.

D. O. Teasley wrote:

Salvation's free, glad joy to all
    Of Adam's fallen race;
We'll tell the story far and near
    Of saving, keeping grace.[1]

---

1. D. Otis Teasley, "A Song of Joy," *Worship the Lord: Hymnal of the Church of God* (Anderson, IN: Warner, 1989), 615.

And in Barney Warren's words:

There's power in the blood to save from sin,
 To bring the peace of God where guilt has been;
A new and happy life will then begin,
 There's power in the blood of Jesus.

No righteousness of ours can e'er avail,
 But through the Lamb of God we shall prevail;
There's power in His blood, all else will fail,
 There's power in the blood of Jesus.

There's power in the blood for our release,
 There's power in the blood to bring soul-peace;
The merits of His blood will not decrease,
 There's power in the blood of Jesus.[2]

 2. We are called to be a **Bible church**. Our preaching, teaching, and practices are to be based on the teachings of the Bible. Anything the Bible as a whole teaches we affirm.
 In Teasley's words:

Back to the blessed old Bible,
 Back at the Master's call,
Back to the words of our Savior,
 Loving, obeying them all.[3]

D. S. Warner put it this way:

By Your blessed Word obeying,
 Lord, we prove our love sincere;
For we hear You gently saying,
 "Love will do as well as hear."

---

2. Barney E. Warren, "Power in the Blood of Jesus," *Worship the Lord*, 425.
3. D. Otis Teasley, "Back to the Blessed Old Bible," *Worship the Lord*, 354.

Dear Redeemer, we would hallow
All your Word, so firm and true,
In Your footsteps meekly follow,
Your commands we love to do.[4]

3. We are called to be a **born-again church**. The truth of the gospel is to transform us into new beings who testify to the saving work of Jesus Christ in our personal lives. In Teasley's words:

When the gospel is preached in the name of the Lord
By the Spirit sent down from above,
My soul thrills with joy at the sound of His word,
For I know in my heart what it means.[5]

Notice the heart language also in other songs. Joseph Fisher begins "I'm Redeemed" with:

I'm redeemed, I'm redeemed,
From the darkness of the night
That so thickly enveloped my soul;
In my heart there have gleamed
Rays of wonderful light,
Where the waves of Thy glory now roll.[6]

Lawrence E. Brooks ends "He Lifted Me Out" with:

I have started for heaven, my heart filled with song,
Wand'ring is over, my sins all are gone;
Thru Jesus own blood cleansed within and without,
O praise His dear name! He lifted me out.[7]

---

4. Daniel S. Warner, "By Your Blessed Word Obeying," *Worship the Lord*, 348.
5. D. Otis Teasley, "I Know in My Heart What It Means," *Worship the Lord*, 417.
6. Joseph C. Fisher, "I'm Redeemed," *Worship the Lord*, 569.
7. Lawrence E. Brooks, "He Lifted Me Out," *Worship the Lord*, 598.

And Warner's song, "There Is Joy in the Service of the Master," includes the following stanza and refrain.

> Could I sing out the pleasure in my bosom,
>> How my heart thrills with glory in the way,
> All the world would no longer in the desert stay,
>> But to my Jesus come, and even today.

> Jesus, my life and my joy evermore,
>> Jesus, forever my heart's deep store:
> Glory to God for redeeming love!
>> O wondrous peace of God that flows from above.[8]

4. We are called to be a **holiness church**. This means that we function with the understanding that the biblical standard is that all believers are called to the whole-hearted love of God and others. Our hymnody is filled with this theme.

Charles Naylor's "Wholehearted Service" says it well, the third stanza and refrain of which goes:

> Since Jesus gave all to redeem me,
>> Since only through mercy I live,
> It now is my joy and my purpose
>> A wholehearted service to give.

> I'll put my whole heart in His service,
>> And do all He asketh of me;
> I mean to live holy and blameless—
>> A Christian indeed will I be.[9]

Lucena Byrum's "A Living Sacrifice" expresses this same theme, the third stanza of which says:

---

8. Daniel S. Warner, "There Is Joy in the Service of the Master," *Worship the Lord*, 614.
9. Charles W. Naylor, "Wholehearted Service," *Worship the Lord*, 515.

No gift, however grand or great,
    Could pay the debt I owe;
I bring myself, my life, my all,
    A living gift bestow.[10]

The first stanza and refrain of Mildred Howard's "Consecration" establishes this theme for the whole song:

Since Jesus gave His life for me
Should I not give Him mine?
I'm consecrated, Lord, to Thee,
I shall be wholly Thine.

My life, O Lord, I give to Thee,
My talents, time and all;
I'll serve Thee, Lord, and faithful be,
I'll hear Thy faintest call.[11]

Warner wrote a petitionary prayer in the form of a song, "Fill Me with Thy Spirit, Lord," that includes many crucial dimensions regarding the sanctified life:

Fill me with Thy Spirit, Lord,
Fully save my longing soul;
Thru the precious cleansing blood
Purify and make me whole.

Fill me with Thy holy light,
I would have a single eye;
Make me perfect in Thy sight,
'Tis Thy will to sanctify.

Fill me with Thy perfect love,
Naught of self would I retain;

---

10. Lucena Byrum, "A Living Sacrifice," *Worship the Lord*, 552.
11. Mildred E. Howard, "Consecration," *Worship the Lord*, 475.

Losing all Thy love to prove,
Lord, I count a happy gain.

Fill me with Thy mighty pow'r,
Father, Son and Spirit, come;
In my soul the unction pour,
Make me ever all Thine own.

Fill me with Thy presence now,
Lord, Thyself in me reveal;
At Thy feet I humbly bow
To receive the holy seal.

Come, O Spirit, seal me Thine,
Come, Thy fullness now bestow;
Let Thy glory in me shine,
Let Thy fire within me glow.[12]

5. We are called to be a **unity church**. Since all who are converted to the Lord Jesus Christ are thereby incorporated into the only church he has, we are to reach our hands in Christian fellowship to all other believers who are in this one and only church. A phrase from Naylor's "The Church's Jubilee" that has made its way into the movement's vernacular is, "We reach our hands in fellowship to ev'ry blood-washed one." The basis for experiencing this unity is the experience of holiness of heart, which, as we have seen above, is the wholehearted love of God and others. This holiness of heart is referred to as entire sanctification or perfect love, and is the basis for the experience of unity in the church.

Warner's "The Bond of Perfectness" is the fullest expression we have of this view. Stanza one begins with:

How sweet this bond of perfectness,
The wondrous love of Jesus!

---

12. Daniel S. Warner, "Fill Me with Thy Spirit, Lord," *Worship the Lord*, 269.

A pure foretaste of heaven's bliss,
O fellowship so precious.

The second stanza praises the Lord:

O praise the Lord for love divine
That binds us all together!
A thousand cords our hearts entwine
Forever and forever.

The third declares: "No pow'r of earth or hell, withal, Can rend us from each other." And the fourth stanza says, "Our souls in fellowship embrace, And live in sweet communion." In the refrain, he refers to how

this perfect love
Unites us all in Jesus!
One heart, and soul, and mind:
We prove the union heaven gave us.[13]

And Naylor's "O Church of God" begins with the words:

The church of God one body is,
One Spirit dwells within;
And all her members are redeemed,
And triumph over sin.

O church of God! I love thy courts,
Thou mother of the free;
Thou blessed home of all the saved,
I dwell content in thee.[14]

6. We are called to be a **kingdom of God church**. The quality of the church's life is to be based on kingdom values. The church

---

13. Daniel S. Warner, "The Bond of Perfectness," *Worship the Lord*, 330.
14. Charles W. Naylor, "O Church of God," *Worship the Lord*, 289.

is to proclaim the good news of the kingdom of God, and is to be the arena in which God does dramatic things as signs of the in-breaking of the kingdom into human history. The church, then, is called to be the community of the kingdom, to serve as herald of the kingdom, and to manifest signs of the kingdom.

Clara Brooks's "What a Mighty God We Serve!" is a song about the reign and rule of God: "He rules o'er all in majesty, From His royal throne on high," and "The raging winds and waves are calm, When He says to them, 'Be still.' " The song ends with:

Our God, to save from sin's control,
Gave His Son a sacrifice;
His grace, abounding in the soul,
Makes the earth a paradise.

What a mighty God we serve!
What a mighty God we serve!
Reigning now above on His throne of love,
What a mighty God we serve![15]

The personalization of the kingdom in our hearts is expressed in Warren's "The Kingdom of Peace," the first and second stanzas and refrain of which are:

There's a theme that is sweet to my mem'ry,
There's a joy that I cannot express,
There's a treasure that gladdens my being,
'Tis the kingdom of God's righteousness.

There's a scene of its grandness before me,
Of its greatness there can be no end;
It is joy, it is peace, it is glory,
In my heart, how these riches do blend!

---

15. Clara M. Brooks, "What a Mighty God We Serve!" *Worship the Lord*, 46.

'Tis a kingdom of peace, it is reigning within,
It shall ever increase in my soul;
We possess it right here when He saves from all sin,
And 'twill last while the ages shall roll.[16]

In Jacob Byers's "He Is Just the Same Today," one finds celebration of the dramatic signs of the kingdom:

Have you ever heard of Jesus,
How He came from heav'n to earth
With a name of mighty virtue,
Tho' by very humble birth?
When the world was held in bondage
Under Satan's dismal sway,
Jesus healed their dread diseases—
He is just the same today.

He is just the same today,
He is just the same today;
Yes, He healed in Galilee,
Set the suff'ring captives free,
And He's just the same today.[17]

7. We are called to be a missionary church. Our Lord's mandate to share the good news with all peoples is for the church in every age and place.

The orientation toward all nations of the earth is clearly set forth in Naylor's "O Praise the Lord, All Ye Nations!" the second stanza of which goes:

O praise the Lord, all ye nations!
Praise Him for His goodness!
For He saveth His people from all their sins,

---

16. Daniel S. Warren, "The Kingdom of Peace," *Worship the Lord*, 481.
17. Jacob W. Byers, "He Is Just the Same Today," *Worship the Lord*, 442.

And preserveth the souls of all who will trust Him;
Praise ye the Lord![18]

The song, however, that presents the missionary mandate with explicit clarity is the one commissioned by the church in the 1950s for what was called the Mid-Century Advance. It is "Together We Go to Make Disciples" by Frederick Shackleton, the refrain of which is:

Together we go to make disciples
for Jesus our Lord in ev'ry land;
We're reaching the lost for Christ, the Savior,
On faraway shores and near at hand.

Together we go to tell our neighbors
The message of Christ, our truest Friend.
All power is His, pow'r in earth and heaven,
And He will be with us to the end.[19]

The Church of God, then, is convinced that in order to be God's faithful church, it must be a gospel church, a Bible church, a born-again church, a holiness church, a unity church, a kingdom church, and a missionary church. This is not a list of options from which we may pick and choose; this is the multidimensional character of the church that is truly of God. When any one of these dimensions is missing, the church is displeasing to God. All seven are interrelated and critical to the health of God's church.

As I said at the beginning of this chapter, many more details of the historic vision will be set forth in the "As Christians, Here We Stand" statement in chapter 5, but these are the overarching themes that encompass all the other particulars.

---

18. Charles W. Naylor, "O Praise the Lord, All Ye Nations!" *Worship the Lord*, 2.
19. Frederick G. Shackleton, "Together We Go to Make Disciples," *Worship the Lord*, 297.

To use some other descriptive words, we are to be:

A good news church,
A good book church,
A new life church,
A fully committed church,
A connecting church,
An eternal values church, and
An outreach church.

And using phrases from songs, books, and slogans from our historical life together, we could define our spiritual DNA in the following way. We are to be

A Gospel Trumpet church,[20]
A What the Bible Teaches church,[21]
A "Where Christian Experience Makes You a Member" church,[22]
A "Wholehearted Service" church,[23]
A "United Church for a Divided World,"[24]
A "Kingdom of Peace" church,[25] and
A "Together We Go to Make Disciples" church.[26]

This, then, is a summary of the kind of church we are called to be.

---

20. The journal edited first of all by Daniel Sidney Warner.
21. A book written by Frederick G. Smith.
22. A slogan used on church signs and in publications.
23. A song written by Charles W. Naylor.
24. The slogan used for many years on *Christian Brotherhood Hour*, the international radio program of the Church of God.
25. A song written by Barney E. Warren.
26. A song written by Frederick G. Shackleton.

CHAPTER 2

Evaluating the Vision

Simply identifying the historic vision is not sufficient. While something may be part of the historic vision, it may be off beam. Two criteria by which we should always evaluate each theme of the vision are the following:

First, is it well rooted in the biblical witness about the nature, work, and function of the church? Are there biblical texts that deal explicitly with this theme?

Second, are the interpretations of these biblical passages shared with other Christians, or are they so obscure that no other Christians would be able to come to the same conclusions? In other words, is it a matter of private interpretation, or is it in the public arena of biblical understandings?

We can rejoice in the fact that the seven components of our historic vision do pass both of these crucial tests. Each component is based on biblical texts having to do explicitly with the subject at hand, and, in each case, Christians other than we have identified it as a biblical emphasis that the church in every age and place needs to preach, teach, and practice.

For each component, then, I shall give at least three major biblical references and attach a paragraph citing at least one example of other Christians who have focused on the same biblical emphasis. The examples given do not imply that the Church of God would see eye to eye with them regarding all of the details of their understandings. That is not the point. The point is that Christians other than we ourselves have seen these same scriptural emphases and have dealt seriously with them.

A Gospel Church
Romans 1:1–17
As verse 16 says, "For I am not ashamed of the gospel; it is the power of God for salvation to everyone who has faith, to the Jew first and also to the Greek."

Galatians 1:1–10
Verse 9: "If anyone proclaims to you a gospel contrary to what you received, let that one be accursed."

Ephesians 1
Verse 13 reminds us: "In him you also, when you had heard the word of truth, the gospel of your salvation, and had believed in him, were marked with the seal of the promised Holy Spirit."

The supreme historical example of other Christians identifying the biblical centrality of the gospel is the sixteenth-century Protestant Reformation led by Martin Luther (1483–1546). Luther was a monk in the Roman Catholic Church. In his day, the legalism imposed by the church obliterated the good news of God's gift of salvation. Luther almost drove himself mad trying to satisfy all of the requirements for being acceptable to God. It was during this time of desperation that the reading of Romans, which sets forth the gospel of God's gift of salvation, liberated him. He learned that those who are justified before God are justified not because of all of their good works but by virtue of God's gift working through their faith. The Protestant Reformation that emerged as a result of Luther's liberating experience of the gospel proclaimed this good news. The central function of the church, then, was understood as being that of a herald of this liberating gospel.

A Bible Church
2 Timothy 3:14–17
Verses 16–17: "All scripture is inspired by God and is useful for teaching, for reproof, for correction, and for training in

righteousness, so that everyone who belongs to God may be proficient, equipped for every good work."

Colossians 4:16
"And when this letter has been read among you, have it read also in the church of the Laodiceans."

Luke 24:13–49
In this account of the risen Lord walking and talking incognito with the Emmaus disciples, verse 27 says this about Jesus: "Then beginning with Moses and all the prophets, he [Jesus] interpreted to them the things about himself in all the scriptures."

When they finally realize that their companion is none other than Jesus, they say to each other: "Were not our hearts burning within us while he was talking to us on the road, while he was opening the scriptures to us?" (v 32).

And, in the account about the risen Christ and the larger company of disciples in Jerusalem still later that night, we learn something more about Jesus and the Scriptures: "Then he [Jesus] said to them, 'These are my words that I spoke to you while I was still with you—that everything written about me in the law of Moses, the prophets, and the psalms must be fulfilled.' Then he opened their minds to understand the scriptures."

In the sixteenth-century reformation the reformer who led the way in reminding the church that it is to be a Bible church was John Calvin (1509–64), leader of the Swiss reformation. The churches in this part of the reformation made some visible changes in their places of worship in order to emphasize this commitment. They moved their pulpits to more central locations so that it was made abundantly clear to the congregations that when they came to church the primary purpose was to learn from Scripture. The preachers even changed from wearing liturgical garments that primarily represented their priestly roles to wearing their teaching robes used in the lecture halls of their schools. The preachers, in the course of weeks and months, preached through whole books of the Bible so that their congregations would develop a more adequate understanding of the message of entire books. Instead of simply going through a ritual of worship during which passages of scripture were read with no explanation, the emphasis now was on not only the reading of scripture but also the explanation of it.

A Born-again Church
John 3:1–10
In verse 3, Jesus says to Nicodemus, "No one can see the kingdom of God without being born from above."

2 Corinthians 5:16–17
The last of these two verses reads: "So if anyone is in Christ, there is a new creation; everything old has passed away; see everything has become new!"

Acts 9: 1–19; 22:6–16; 26:12–18
These are the three accounts in Acts about Paul's conversion on the Road to Damascus. In 26:17–18, he hears the Lord say, "I will rescue you from your people and from the Gentiles—to whom I am sending you to open their eyes so that they may turn from darkness to light and from the power of Satan to God, so that they may receive forgiveness of sins and a place among those who are sanctified by faith in me."

The revival and camp meeting movements during the eighteenth and nineteenth centuries and the mass evangelism movements of the twentieth are prime examples of this biblical emphasis on conversion from the old life of sin to new life in Christ. Preachers such as Jonathan Edwards (1703–58), George Whitefield (1714–70), Barton W. Stone (1772–1844), and Charles G. Finney (1792–1875) stand out as leaders of the revival and camp meeting movements. And the names of Billy Sunday (1863–1935) and Billy Graham (b. 1918) are synonymous with mass evangelism in the twentieth century. All of these movements emphasized not only that people should hear the Scriptures read, preached, and taught, but that they should be transformed by the message.

It is not simply a matter of learning about Scripture but a matter of being changed by it. The goal of preaching is not merely that people have more head knowledge at the end of the message, but that people will be born again. Life transformation is the goal.

A Holiness Church
Acts 2:1–4
Verses 2 and 3: "And suddenly from heaven there came a sound like the rush of a violent wind, and it filled the entire house where they were sitting. Divided tongues, as of fire, appeared among them, and a tongue rested on each of them."

1 Thessalonians 5:23–24
Verse 23 of this benediction: "May the God of peace himself sanctify you entirely; and may your spirit and soul and body be kept sound and blameless at the coming of our Lord Jesus Christ."

Romans 12:1–2
"I appeal to you therefore, brothers and sisters, by the mercies of God, to present your bodies as a living sacrifice, holy and acceptable to God, which is your spiritual worship. Do not be conformed to this world, but be transformed by the renewing of your minds, so that you may discern what is the will of God—what is good and acceptable and perfect."

1 John 4: 7–21
Verse 17 says: "Love has been perfected among us in this: that we may have boldness on the day of judgment, because as he is, so are we in this world."

This was the emphasis of the eighteenth-century Wesleyan Revival led by John Wesley (1703–1791), which continued in the nineteenth-century Holiness Movement in the United States. Wesley, faithful Anglican that he was, found it disturbing that nominally Christian people disregarded the clear teachings of Scripture that we are called to the perfection of love for God and for others. He did not understand this perfect love as flawlessness, but as wholehearted devotion to God and to the well-being of others. In the Anglican Church, a prayer that was regularly offered was, "Almighty God, unto whom all hearts are open and all desires known, cleanse the thoughts of our hearts by the inspiration of Thy Holy Spirit that we may perfectly love Thee and worthily magnify Thy holy name, through Jesus Christ our Lord. Amen." Week after week, nominal Christians prayed that God would work within them so that they would "perfectly love" God, but week after week, they disregarded what that perfect love meant. They gave little evidence of the wholehearted love of God and others. Wesley sought to change this. The Holiness Movement that emerged in the United States emphasized this same concern. The vigorous message to all Christians was that God calls all believers to the wholehearted love of God and others. This is not just for those who are especially religious; it is for all believers without exception.

A Unity Church
John 17:20–26
Verses 20–21 contain the essence of our Lord's high priestly prayer: "I ask not only on behalf of these, but also on behalf of those who will believe in me through their work, that they may all be one. As you, Father, are in me and I am in you, may they also be in us, so that the world may believe that you have sent me."

1 Corinthians 12:12–31
Verse 13 reads: "For in the one Spirit we were all baptized into one body—Jews or Greeks, slave or free—and we were all made to drink of one Spirit."

Ephesians 4:1–16
The first six verses serve as the clarion call to Christian unity: "I, therefore, the prisoner in the Lord beg you to lead a life worthy of the calling to which you have been called, with all humility and gentleness, with patience, bearing with one another in love

making every effort to maintain the unity of the Spirit in the bond of peace. There is one body and one Spirit, just as you were called to the one hope of your calling, one Lord, one faith, one baptism, one God and Father of all, who is above all and through all and in all."

The early-nineteenth-century Restorationist Movement, under the father and son leadership of Thomas (1763–1854) and Alexander Campbell (1788–1866), was motivated by the unity themes of the New Testament. The Campbells were weary with all of the denominational infighting, competition, and building of divisive structures. They were convinced that God has only one church and that it is our responsibility to function in such a way that we give expression to that reality. In order to do that it was necessary to return to the standards of the Bible and live according to what was found there. For too long the church had disregarded the mandates for church unity found in Scripture. It was time to take those seriously by dealing with the practicalities of how to go about being one church.

A Kingdom of God Church
Matthew is often referred to as the Gospel of the Kingdom. In 6:10, Jesus teaches the church to pray "Your kingdom come. Your will be done, on earth as it is in heaven." According to 9:35, he "went about all the cities and villages, teaching in their synagogues, and proclaiming the good news of the kingdom, and curing every disease and every sickness."

And the promise in 24:14 is, "This good news of the kingdom will be proclaimed throughout the world, as a testimony to all the nations; and then the end will come."

Luke 9:1–2
"Then Jesus called the twelve together and gave them power and authority over all demons and to cure diseases, and he sent them out to proclaim the kingdom of God and to heal."

Romans 14:17
"For the kingdom of God is not food and drink but righteousness and peace and joy in the Holy Spirit."

The Anabaptists of the sixteenth century took seriously what it means to live according to the values of the kingdom. Contemporary examples of churches growing out of the Anabaptist movement are the Mennonites, the Brethren churches, and the Amish. It is their understanding that the church is called to be a kingdom church here and now. They understand the Sermon on the Mount (Matt 5–7) to be the standard for the way the church is to function at the present time. This is the reason so much attention is given to the practicalities of daily life, war and peace, attitudes and values, and the Christian's relationship to the civil order and to the world in general. They deal with all of these matters because of their conviction that Scripture calls the church to be a kingdom of God church here and now.

A Missionary Church
Matthew 28:18–20
The last two verses are: "Go therefore and make disciples of all nations, baptizing them in the name of the Father and of the Son and of the Holy Spirit, and teaching them to obey everything that I have commanded you."

Acts 1:8; 2:1–4, 37–47
According to 1:8, our risen Lord promises: "But you will receive power when the Holy Spirit has come upon you; and you will be my witnesses in Jerusalem, in all Judea and Samaria, and to the ends of the earth."

Romans 1:14–16
After expressing his "eagerness to proclaim the gospel to you also who are in Rome, Paul then says: "For I am not ashamed of the gospel; it is the power of God for salvation to everyone who has faith, to the Jew first and also to the Greek."

One historical example of this biblical emphasis is the Protestant missionary enterprise associated with such well-known missionaries as the Congregationalist John Eliot (1604–90) to North American Indians; the Baptist William Carey (1761–1834) to India, and Adoniram Judson (1788–1850) to Burma; the independent David Livingstone (1813–73) to Africa; and the Wesleyan J. Hudson Taylor (1832–1905) to China. These and hundreds of others went at great personal sacrifice to people very unlike themselves in terms of culture and ethnicity because they were convinced that the church was under divine mandate to share the good news of God's salvation in Jesus Christ with all peoples. They were convinced that the missionary mandate had not been fulfilled by the original apostles, as some taught. Neither was it a curious piece of scripture that could be treated lightly as though it were optional. The missionary mandate was given by our Lord and was to be obeyed until his return at the end of the age. Therefore, the church was under divine mandate to send and support missionaries. Obviously this meant that some of its sons and daughters would have to make the radical sacrifice of leaving home and going to faraway lands for the sake of fulfilling this mandate.

Each of these seven dimensions of our historic vision is well rooted in Scripture. Furthermore, each has been emphasized by other Christians. Each of them is a part of the DNA of the wider Christian tradition. But we may be the only fellowship of Christians in which all seven of these are vigorously and persistently lifted up as requiring sustained emphasis in preaching, teaching, and practice. (I would rejoice to be proven wrong.)

It is this configuration of emphases that makes up our particular DNA as a movement. The distinctive character of the Church of God is that all seven of these emphases have found a home in one and the same group of Christians, and have been formative in the way we go about being church. As we reflect on our life together and on our calling under God, these seven themes interact with and inform each other. The seven are the fabric of our living, thinking, and acting. None is viewed as optional or as the special domain of other Christians but not necessarily for us. No, we are convinced that the health of the whole church depends on being both informed and formed by all of these scriptural themes.

When we find ourselves in a circle of Christians where any one of these themes is marginalized, we are called to bring it from the margins to the center of what it means to be a God-pleasing church. That, I believe, is our God-ordained role. Whether we fulfill that role or abandon it, the fact remains that the seven are biblical emphases. I believe, therefore, that the God who inspired Scripture continues calling on his people to preach, teach, and practice all seven of these biblical emphases.

Let us turn now to the basic assumptions regarding the church that is to have these emphases in its life and ministry. In the next two chapters, we will deal with the theological framework within which these things are said about the church.

CHAPTER 3

Articulating the Vision

It is theologically illustrative that D. S. Warner separated himself from a denomination known as the Churches of God and identified with a movement called simply "the church of God." The singular form has identified us ever since. Warner had identified with the concept of the church set forth in the writings of Paul where the emphasis is on the oneness, the universality, the singularity of the church. Warner understood from Paul that the universal church is not the sum total of local congregations. Rather, the universal church is the one body of Christ: "For in the one Spirit we were all baptized into one body—Jews or Greeks, slave or free—and we were all made to drink of one Spirit" (1 Cor 12:13). Therefore, in our understanding of the universal church, we are not to think of it as the *end* of an equation of local churches. Instead, we are to begin with the universal church and think of each local congregation as being an expression of the one universal church.

To be converted to Christ is to be incorporated into the one universal church. One is not converted and then invited to join a local church. Rather, when one is converted, one is then and there joined with the one universal church. We become a member of the only church God has. In Warner's song "The Lord Our Shepherd," stanza 2 begins with "The sheep of his pasture are one, Yea, one as the Father and Son."[1] Other songwriters also pick up on this theme. Charles Naylor begins his song "O Church of God" with the declaration of this truth:

---

1. Daniel S. Warner, "The Lord Our Shepherd," *Worship the Lord: Hymnal of the Church of God* (Anderson, IN: Warner Press, 1989), 661.

"The church of God one body is, One Spirit dwells within; And all her members are redeemed, And triumph over sin."[2] And D. O. Teasley in the first and fourth stanzas of "Church of the Living God" sets forth the position well:

Church of the Living God,
    The pillar of the truth,
Thou dost enclose within thy walls
    The aged and the youth;
Here in thy light of love,
    The saints with gladness meet;
Here ev'ry tribe and kindred come
    In fellowship so sweet.

Church of the Living God,
    Thy saints are born of love;
In heaven's golden book of life
    Their names are kept above:
And God shall guard His own,
    Preserve them by His grace,
And naught but sin against the Lord
    Shall e'er their names erase.[3]

Is it possible to put the historic vision of the Church of God into one short sentence? I believe it is. Below is my attempt to do so.

We are called by God to live out, by the power of the Holy Spirit[4], what it means to be an expression of God's one universal church, in harmony with New Testament emphases.[5]

---

2. Charles W. Naylor, "O Church of God," *Worship the Lord*, 289.
3. D. Otis Teasley, "Church of the Living God," *Worship the Lord*, 281.
4. See more on the church as the fellowship of the Holy Spirit in chapter 4.
5. The reference here is to the seven dimensions of the historical vision set forth earlier: a gospel church, a Bible church, a born-again church, a holiness church, a unity church, a kingdom of God church, and a missionary church.

This movement came into existence in the late nineteenth century with a particular vision of what it means to be the church. One of the questions often asked in the earlier days was: "Have you seen the church?" A common testimony was, "I've seen the church." Conversation about newcomers to the fellowship included such comments as: "He's been with us for a while but I don't believe he has really ever seen the church," or "It wasn't long after she came among us when she really saw the church."

People often referred to seeing the church as a personal revelation. By such language they testified to having come to the realization that God has only one church, and that it is made up of everyone who is born of God. When they testified in such a way, they were not referring to being convinced to join a certain denomination; neither were they referring to this particular movement of Christians. Instead, they were referring to being led by the Holy Spirit to the reality that in the New Testament there is only one church, and it includes everyone who is born again. When people testified to "seeing the church," they meant that they saw God's one and only universal church. They rejoiced about being in it by virtue of their faith in Jesus Christ, and they rejoiced that every other person both past and present possessing the same saving faith is in it, also.

From that point on, their church life took on new significance. Their purpose was to live out the reality of that one, universal church. Not only was that the life principle of individual believers, but it was the organizing principle for local congregations. The question for each local congregation was, How do we go about being a gathering that demonstrates the biblical characteristics of the one, universal church?

The crucially defining question for us at the crossroads is this: Have we seen the church? And, if so, do we intend to live it out? And do we intend to remain faithful to the call of God to be an expression of his one universal church, in harmony with New Testament emphases?

In order for the Church of God as a whole to be faithful to this call, some guidelines are critically important:

- We must be good stewards of the historic vision. (More on this in chapters 8–10.)

- We must attend to the practicalities of living it out. (More on this in chapter 11.)

- We must preach and teach the vision with regularity. (More on this in chapters 6 and 7.)

- We must serve as a laboratory in which we learn and practice all seven of the major biblical emphases about the church. (More on this in chapter 7.)

- We must share with other Christians and Christian fellowships the call for them to do the same. (More on this in chapter 12.)

- We must live as the servant people of God for the sake of his mission in the world and for the well-being of all God's people. (More on this in the Conclusion.)

CHAPTER 4

Receiving Empowerment for the Vision

Empowerment to live authentically as the church begins with the conviction that the vision is of God, and not merely of human origin. Is it God's will for the church to be a gospel church? A Bible church? A born-again church? A holiness church? A unity church? A kingdom of God church? A missionary church? Can we make a case that God is indifferent as to whether even one of these dimensions is missing? If not, are we convinced that neither can we be indifferent about any one of the dimensions? Apart from such conviction, a church simply will not have the spiritual fortitude for bringing the vision to fulfillment.

The experience of empowerment, however, must move beyond mere conviction to an openness to the work of the Holy Spirit among us, corporately and individually, and then move on to obedience. Since the Holy Spirit is the author, preserver, and interpreter of Scripture, the same Holy Spirit will empower those who preach, teach, and live out the message of Scripture. Furthermore, the same Spirit will work creatively among us to give expression to the biblical message.

The Church of God, from the beginning, has been devoted to the New Testament standard of being a fellowship of the Holy Spirit. The Holy Spirit calls us, empowers us, sanctifies us, endows us with gifts, superintends our life together, places us in the body according to his purpose, sends us forth on the divine mission, interprets Scripture, leads us into all truth, establishes us as kingdom people here and now, gives us a foretaste of heaven, and blesses us with his continuous presence.

Charles Naylor expresses in song the nature of the church as the fellowship of the Spirit:

> The church of God one body is,
>   One Spirit dwells within;
> And all her members are redeemed,
>   And triumph over sin.
>
> Divinely built, divinely ruled
>   To God she doth submit;
> His will her law, His truth her guide,
>   Her path is glory-lit.
>
> God sets her members each in place,
>   According to His will—
> Apostles, prophets, teachers, all,
>   His purpose to fulfill.
>
> In beauty stand, O church of God,
>   With righteousness arrayed;
> Put on thy strength and face thy foes
>   With courage undismayed.
>
> O church of God! I love thy courts,
>   Thou mother of the free;
> Thou blessed home of all the saved,
>   I dwell content in thee.[1]

The church as the place of the Spirit is the place where individuals experience the Pentecostal outpouring of the Holy Spirit. W. J. Henry's "Let the Fire Fall on Me" is a supreme example:

---

1. Charles W. Naylor, "O Church of God," *Worship the Lord: Hymnal of the Church of God* (Anderson, IN: Warner Press, 1989), 289.

Lord, I would be wholly Thine,
   I would do Thy will divine,
From the world and sin and self I would be free;
   On the altar now I lie,
And with all my heart I cry,
   Let the holy fire from heaven fall on me.

I would have sufficient grace
   Ev'ry foe to bravely face,
And an overcomer evermore to be;
   That I well may fill my place,
And that I may win the race,
   Let the holy fire from heaven fall on me.

Holy Spirit from above,
   Fill my longing soul with love,
Till the Master's image all in me may see;
   Make me gentle, true and kind,
Meek of heart and humble mind,
   Let the holy fire from heaven fall on me.

In the kingdom I would stay,
   There to labor night and day,
Any way and anywhere Thy will may be;
   But that I may do my best,
And that others may be blest,
   Let the holy fire from heaven fall on me.

Let the fire fall on me,
   Let the fire fall on me;
The fire of Pentecost, consuming sin and dross,
   Let the holy fire from heaven fall on me.[2]

And the refrain of Charles Naylor's "Spirit Holy" expresses the believer's prayer:

---

2. William J. Henry, "Let the Fire Fall on Me," *Worship the Lord*, 483.

Spirit holy, Spirit holy,
    All my being now possess;
Lead me, rule me, work within me,
    Through my life Thy will express.[3]

As a fellowship of the Holy Spirit, then, it seems to me that three basic questions face us regarding our historic vision:

- Are we convinced by the Holy Spirit that this is the biblical vision regarding a church that is pleasing to God?

- Are we, therefore, persuaded by the Holy Spirit that these emphases are essential for the well-being of the church in any age, any place, any circumstance—for long established churches and for recent church plants; for small congregations and for megachurches, and all those in between; for very traditional churches and for those committed to newer ways of doing things?

- Are we intentionally and prayerfully availing ourselves of the power of the Holy Spirit as we preach, teach, and live out this biblical vision?

A negative answer to any one of these questions will mean that we'll settle for rummaging around among the dusty artifacts of our historical life together. That is to say, we will become satisfied merely to read the old literature, listen to the oral history, and examine our predecessors' memorabilia, such as houses and pictures and furniture. To be sure, we may profit greatly from learning about the commendable values reflected by their lives in the past, and may enjoy laughing at the oddities that we come

---

3. Charles W. Naylor "Spirit Holy," *Worship the Lord*, 267.

across. It is good to know the stories of our religious ancestors and to laugh at their oddities, but that isn't enough.

Empowerment for the realization of the vision requires our earnest conviction that we are dealing with nothing less than biblical perspectives and that these perspectives are mandatory for the health of the church in all ages and in all places and circumstances.

Empowerment requires our sincere prayers for the creative, invigorating, guiding, and sustaining work of the Holy Spirit as we preach, teach, and live out the vision.

Empowerment requires our earnest conviction that the Holy Spirit calls us to embrace this divine agenda.

Empowerment requires our openness to and anticipation of the work of the Holy Spirit.

Empowerment requires our fervent prayer for discerning the Spirit's specific directions about what we are to do.

Empowerment requires our humble dedication to living out this Spirit-inspired vision.

CHAPTER 5

Celebrating the Vision

From the very beginning, songs have been our primary means for celebrating the vision of God's church. These songs were written from within the fellowship of the church. As poets and musicians reflected on the message being preached, taught, and written about, they expressed it in poems and songs so that the wider fellowship could celebrate it.

The contemporary church is at a crossroads regarding how we go about celebrating the vision. The challenge facing us is at least fivefold.

Challenge 1: To introduce the heritage songs to those who do not know them, preferably by those who sing them well. This provides a pleasant experience when people hear these songs for the first time. Our musicians should not have to figure out how to sing songs that were written in a style very different from contemporary music. The singing of heritage songs should never be done in such a way that it elevates those who know them above those who do not. In all cases we need to avoid pride of knowledge, and call no attention whatsoever to those who know them as over against those who do not. Good manners are the key.

Challenge 2: To update the music of the heritage songs so that those who do not know this kind of music can learn the songs in a style that is more in keeping with the way people sing today.

Challenge 3: To keep the historic vision before the church so that the contemporary poets and musicians in the church will have a theological context for their inspiration.

Challenge 4: To encourage new poetic and musical expressions of the historic vision. (More on this in chapter 7).

Challenge 5: To develop worship resources, other than music, which use Scriptural passages that are the basis for our historic vision.

It is to this fifth challenge that I now turn. In *Church of God at the Crossroads*, I developed what I called "A Confession of Christian Faith According to Scripture."[1] It was my personal attempt to express in the words of Scripture the major emphases of the Church of God. Following the publication of the book, one of my projects was to test whether I got it right in that Confession. In order to do that, I consulted with church leaders around the world,[2] and on the basis of those conversations, revised it into a more adequate expression of the church's faith according to Scripture. In Appendix 1, you will find what I am convinced is our collective understanding of the Christian faith, using Scriptural words to express it.

But how can this confession of faith can be used? First, it can be printed in a brochure as a scripturally based introduction of ourselves. Second, the Introduction and Part I can be used as a component of worship in one service, and each of the other three parts in three successive services. Third, the whole confession can form the framework of a single service. See Appendix 2 for an example of one such service. Obviously, many other possibilities for building such a service can be developed, but this is offered as a stimulus for additional creative expressions.

---

1. Gilbert W. Stafford, *Church of God at the Crossroads* (Anderson, IN: Warner Press, 2000), 90–93.
2. See the note in Appendix 1 for a list of meetings.

CHAPTER 6

Preaching the Vision

Often I am asked how we can regain a sense of unifying purpose in the church. My response is always the same: preaching the vision. Unless preachers catch the vision, it is unlikely that the church, in general, will even know what the vision is, and the celebration of it in songs and other corporate celebrations will be little more than the rattling of the bones of the past.

Many options exist for planning one's preaching program. Some follow a selection of biblical texts chosen in consultation with a wide-range of Christians so that in the course of three years the themes of the whole Bible are covered. This is called the Common Lectionary. For each Sunday of the year, a Psalm, another Old Testament passage, a New Testament passage from other than the Gospels, and a passage from one of the Gospels are selected. These four selections have a common theme. The preacher may focus on the common theme of all four passages or choose one of the selections for the sermon.

Other preachers use the Uniform Series of Scripture lessons for this purpose. This has the advantage of tracking along with the Bible texts in our Sunday school curriculum.

Still other preachers plan their preaching program around themes that they sense need emphasis in the congregation, or around themes of the year. Others work simply on a week-to-week basis, developing sermons that grow directly out of their discernment of what the Lord would have them say at that particular time.

All of these have their strengths and weaknesses.

Whichever approach is used, it can be enriched, I believe, by including from time to time a preaching emphasis on the biblical vision of the church. One might, for instance, preach a series of sermons on the seven biblical emphases: being a gospel church, a Bible church, a born-again church, a holiness church, a unity church, a kingdom of God church, and a missionary church.

Another approach would be to preach through the texts included in "As Christians, Here We Stand." In discussions with pastors around the world concerning this document, I often heard comments such as: "Yes, those are important biblical passages, and yes, they are passages that have been lifted up in the preaching, teaching, and writing of the Church of God. But for some reason I have never preached on those passages."

Two possibilities for developing preaching series according to the two approaches just discussed are set forth in Appendix 3.

We are not talking here merely about Church of God emphases. We are talking about *biblical* emphases. We should preach these not as Church of God emphases but as *biblical* emphases. In fact, their identification with the Church of God need never be mentioned, because we should not leave the impression that such a series is a narrow, denominational series. When we overemphasize the Church of God connection, some among us are likely to tune us out until we return to preaching what they might consider "the nondenominational stuff." It is important to focus primarily on Scripture so that everybody present is called to come to terms with what *Scripture* teaches.

Unless preachers in congregations of all sizes and places are inspired to preach these biblical themes, there simply is no hope for addressing our lack of unifying purpose. No amount of institutional fine-tuning will be able to address the doctrinal malaise among us. It will be sufficiently addressed only as we preachers

- Catch the biblical vision,

- Develop it with interpretive integrity,

- Proclaim it with passion born of the Holy Spirit, and

- Present it not as Church of God in-house themes but as biblical themes intended by God for the whole church.

Then, and only then, will the fires of truth ignite our life as a fellowship. Only then will our togetherness be transformed into living out what it means to be an expression of the one universal church. Only then will we be good stewards of the biblical marks of what it means to be a church that is pleasing to God. Only then will we fulfill our role in the economy of God for the renewal and reformation of the whole church.

I find some young seminarians ready to do the above, and some seasoned ministers are already doing it. The question is whether it will happen all across the church. Will preachers in little churches do it? Will preachers in megachurches do it? Will preachers in church plants do it? Will preachers in old, well-established churches do it? Will preachers in each and every ethnic group do it? Will preachers in churches that have very tenuous relations with the wider fellowship do it? Will those who teach preaching in our schools help students learn how to do it?

Will we, in fact, have a church-wide preaching festival that celebrates what it means to be a gospel church, a Bible church, a born-again church, a holiness church, a unity church, a kingdom of God church, a missionary church?

Our future together depends on the answers we give to the questions above.

CHAPTER 7

Teaching the Vision

We teach the vision by preaching it.
In the previous chapter, the importance of doing this was stated and two possible preaching programs were set forth. Without effective preaching, the other methods of teaching set forth below are not likely to succeed. Preaching is the linchpin in the whole endeavor.

We teach the vision by singing it.
In chapter 5 I gave several suggestions about how to use the heritage music, and stated the importance of developing new music. The poetic and musical juices continue to flow in the Church of God. But in order for the poets and songwriters to do their part, preachers and teachers have to provide a robust theological environment within which the they can find inspiration and direction for the themes they develop and the approaches taken. (See chapter 6.)

As the church produces new songs, learns them, and sings them, the vision will be taught in contemporary singing styles.

We teach the vision by having classes on it.
Church of God Ministries has developed curricular materials that spell out the historic vision, materials that can be used for the Sunday school as well as for leadership development, interest groups, youth meetings, and introductory sessions for new participants in the church.[1] Classes provide the environment in which questions

---

1. Visit the Church of God publishing house, Warner Press, Inc., at www.warnerpress.org. Click on the tab labeled "Church of God."

can be asked, explanations given, information provided, and the opportunity is given for the vision to be caught.

It is important for us to remind ourselves that we have the responsibility not only to lead people into an experience of the saving grace of God, but also into an experience of the sanctifying grace of God. Furthermore, it is our responsibility to lead people into an understanding of what it means to be church. What does it mean for a local congregation to be an expression of the one universal church of God? When we stop dealing seriously with that question, we abandon our historic role in the body of Christ. We need to deal with that issue not only with adults but also with young people. Dr. Robert H. Reardon, president emeritus of Anderson University, reminds us that in its early days, very young people led the Church of God reformation movement. We need to remember that the historic vision is not just for old-timers; since it is a vision rooted in the Bible which is for old and young alike, it is, therefore, for people of all ages.

While it is absolutely necessary that teachers and other leaders in the church be believers, and have expertise and gifts for their work in the life of the church, that is not enough. They also need to be informed by the historic vision. Only then will they be in a position to contribute to the mission of the Church of God, namely, to live out what it means to be an expression of God's one universal church, in harmony with New Testament emphases.

One of the greatest challenges facing the whole church of Jesus Christ today is the issue of what it means to be church. Who are we? How are we as the church supposed to function? What are we supposed to be doing? That challenge faces the Church of God as well. Dealing with this issue at every level of our instructional ministries is mandatory if we as the Church of God are to do what we are called by God to do, namely, to live out being a fellowship of the one universal church.

We teach the vision by confessing it in services of worship.
I have developed a resource for use in worship, consisting of a broad range of biblical emphases. This resource, called "As

Christians, Here We Stand," expresses the theological texture of our historical life together.[2] It is intended as a way for the people of God as a whole to celebrate what we preach and teach. Even as our heritage songs were born within the environment of preaching, teaching, and writing, and provided a way for the people of God to say Amen to the biblical truth set forth in that preaching, teaching, and writing, even so this resource is intended for the same purpose. It is another way whereby the people of God can say Amen to the proclamation of the truth. It sets forth a rather comprehensive range of texts and emphases that provide the texture of who we are in God's household, so that we will not be as likely to forget those texts and emphases. Furthermore, when outsiders ask "What do you people believe?" and when insiders ask "What do we as a fellowship believe?" the "As Christians, Here We Stand" is one way of answering the questions.

We teach the vision by facilitating personal stories about it.
As a boy growing up in the church, I remember times when people newly associated with us would testify to "seeing the church." They would share the new insight they had about the church being made up of all who are born-again. They would tell about their new understanding that the only way into it is the new birth. They would rejoice that to be a Christian is thereby to be a member of the only church God has. They would express excitement about the new challenge of being with a fellowship that was taking seriously what it means to be a local expression of the one universal church of God. While those personal stories always ran the risk of crossing the line into a kind of spiritual pride, in my experience they came across, for the most part, as genuine expressions of gratitude for being the beneficiaries of a refreshingly biblical understanding of what it means to be church. Furthermore, as a boy growing up in this testimonial environment, I was learning something about the one universal church. It was more than just an idea that my father preached; it was something that people were actually experiencing. I think that in the present such testimonies would still be beneficial

---

2. Discussed in chapter 5, this resource can be found in Appendix 1.

so long as they avoid the pitfalls of spiritual pride, of ugliness toward other Christians, and of a smug attitude that we are the only people God has and that all must come to us. To fall into any of those pitfalls is to lose sight of the vision of what it means to be an expression of the one universal church of God. The point of the testimony is the biblical truth about the church, not the Church of God reformation movement as such. We are called to be good stewards of this biblical truth, not substitutes for it. It is the biblical truth about the nature of the one universal church to which we call the people of God, not to us. It is the joy of living out the truth that should be uppermost in our personal stories, not the joy of merely associating with us. To the extent that testimonies avoid the above pitfalls, and to the extent that they focus on biblical truth and one's joy in it, to that extent testimonies can be powerful teaching tools.

We teach the vision by developing banners about it.
Many churches now use banners in their places of worship. The making of banners for use in church buildings including the place of worship can in and of itself be an excellent teaching tool. For instance, a series of banners could be made, one each for the seven historic emphases. A series of seven banners might include wording something like:

> *Pinehurst Church: A Gospel church*
> *Pinehurst Church: A Bible church*
> *Pinehurst Church: A Born-again church*
> *Pinehurst Church: A Holiness church*
> *Pinehurst Church: A Unity church*
> *Pinehurst Church: A Kingdom church*
> *Pinehurst Church: A Missionary church*

These banners could be exhibited in connection with the pastor's preaching program on these same themes, and, depending on the space available, might be left as the pastor moves from one theme to others, so that at the end of the series all seven banners would be on display in the place of worship.

Another possibility is to use historic terminology:

Pinehurst Church: Led by the Gospel Trumpet
Pinehurst Church: Discovering What the Bible Teaches
Pinehurst Church: Where Christian Experience Makes You a Member
Pinehurst Church: Called to Wholehearted Service
Pinehurst Church: A United Church for a Divided World
Pinehurst Church: Living in the Kingdom of Peace
Pinehurst Church: Together We Go to Make Disciples

Another possibility is to develop several banners around this one theme: "Called to be a fellowship of God's whole church in this place."

My aim here is simply to illustrate the use of banners and to encourage the creative juices to flow among others.

We teach the vision by practical holiness in our daily conversations, activities, and attitudes.

People learn as much, if not more, from our daily manner of life than from our sermons, lessons, and writings. Learning takes place as persons observe how we live out our answers to questions such as these:

- Do we share in the natural contexts of our lives our gratitude for the grace of God?

- Do we read Scripture regularly, prayerfully reflect on it, and share insights gained and guidance received for daily life?

- Do we have a personal testimony about the forgiving and redeeming grace of God in our lives, and are we willing to share it when the time is right?

- Do we order the activities of our lives according to what God has called us to be and do?

- Do we talk about all Christians as our dearly beloved brothers and sisters in Christ?

- Do we struggle with the challenging implications of living out kingdom values both in the personal decisions we make as well as in our participation in and discussion of family, civic, national, and international issues?

- Do we function as active participants in the church's missionary enterprise, whether in leading or in supportive roles?

We teach the vision by publishing it.
The Church of God reformation movement began as a publication endeavor focused in the work of the Gospel Trumpet Company. While the publication enterprise of the church is diminished from what it was in an earlier period, the need for publication, nevertheless, remains. We can rejoice at a renewed commitment in this area. It is only when theological perspectives find their way into the printed books, journals, tracts, and articles as well as into the newer medium of Internet websites that it becomes a reference point for those who are interested in what we have to say. Putting our understandings into hard copy disciplines us to say it well, and it provides a solid reference point for others to enter into conversation with us. Leaving perspectives strictly to an oral tradition is the recipe for degeneration, whereas putting it into written form leads to refinement.

Publication provides us with the opportunity to be critiqued by those who see things differently, but it also makes our contributions more available to the wider church. Our theologians, historians, biblical scholars, and other persons in our colleges and seminary need to continue writing about the vision, and publishing. Our preachers, songwriters, teachers, poets, and storytellers also need to continue doing the same.

But it is not enough to produce lots of material. The big question is how it is promoted in the public market. The point of writing and publishing is not so that our writers can have the satisfaction of having some of their work in published form. Nor is it simply for the satisfaction of the in-group of the church. We need to move to a completely different level in this area, and that is how to market our materials for the benefit of the wider church. In my view, we have been far, far too timid in this respect. We have been distracted by a survival mentality, and not well informed as to the value of what we publish for the wider church. We have been satisfied with writing and publishing for a Church of God reformation movement market, rather than for a Christian market. We need to have a major paradigm change regarding this. Our songs and books should not be thought of as simply for us. If they are not for the wider church we will be involved simply in an in-house private discourse rather than in a public discourse in the church at large. Furthermore, if our publications are simply for us, we will not have the benefit of the critique of the wider church, and they will not take us seriously.

We teach the vision by developing congregational laboratories for it.
I think that we have not been as intentional about this as we ought to be. A laboratory is a place where explorations are made, and the results made available for the benefit of those beyond the laboratory.

Many of my Christian friends outside our particular ranks are very interested in knowing how a church functions without requiring people to join either a local organization or a denominational structure. I once heard a representative of the Episcopal Church say in an ecumenical gathering that the churches represented there had a lot to learn from the approach we typically make to church membership.

I have found remarkable interest on the part of ecumenical people in how a church functions when it takes seriously the relationship between holiness and unity.

I have been with Anabaptists who, as people with great interest in kingdom themes, ask probing questions about how these themes relate to holiness and evangelism.

I think that we do not have an adequate appreciation of the particular mix of biblical themes that have historically informed us. We have, it seems to me, one of the most challenging, engaging, and exhilarating callings imaginable. How, then, can we go about being church in a way that takes seriously our call to be an expression of the one universal church of God? Answering that question in the laboratory includes how a congregation goes about being multiracial, multiethnic, cross-generational, cross-cultural, cross-economic. How do we go about taking the message of the Bible seriously in our time and place?

What does congregational life look like when the seven themes of our historic vision are emphasized? How is each of the themes impacted by the others? What kind of spiritual formation takes place in a church where all of these themes are taught, preached, and celebrated? What do we learn about these matters that may be of benefit to the wider church? How do we go about compiling the data from our many laboratories so that we can formulate insights about church life having these particular values and perspectives?

In many respects we are an historic experiment. The data are still coming in. One might say that we are called to be the Church of God Experimental Laboratory: we are learning how in this time and place to live out, by the power of the Holy Spirit, what it means to be an expression of the one universal church, in harmony with New Testament emphases.

CHAPTER 8

Equipping an Ordained Ministry
for the Vision

My father, D. C. Stafford, celebrated his eighty-fifth birthday in November 2001. Over the course of his ministry he was the founding pastor of two churches and the pastor of six others. After retirement, he served some twenty churches as interim pastor, and until recent years served in an associate role in another congregation. His has been a long and fruitful ministry. Both my brother Rod, who is a pastor, and I owe much to him in terms of basic values and understandings of the Christian ministry. He is a man of integrity, wisdom, skill, and knowledge. I am grateful to be in ordained ministry with him. I am humbled by the quality of his work. I am aware of many, many ways in which I fall far below the standards of his work. I am proud to be one of his sons.

Dad is a high school graduate. He has no formal schooling beyond that. He was committed to being equipped for the Christian ministry, although it took place in a different way than was the case for Rod and me. The components of Dad's equipping process included the following.

He bought lots of books and read them. Spending a significant amount of time daily in his study was standard. His Bibles and books were marked; comments were written in the margins; notes were made on the back pages. During the whole time of his pastoral ministry he preached twice on Sundays, often led a mid-week service, and sometimes taught a Sunday school class. It is significant that his room, whether at the church or at home, was called a study. That was the right word for it because it was primarily a place for prayerful preparation to preach and teach, not primarily a center for church administration.

Second, the *Gospel Trumpet* (and later *Vital Christianity*) was a standard piece of his mail. Here again, he read them from cover to cover, marked the articles, and clipped some for his reference file. Reading that journal provided regular inspiration, information, and doctrinal instruction.

Third, he attended camp meetings during the summer, sometimes as many as three or so in one season. Much of the preaching in those meetings was doctrinal. Other benefits of camp meetings included the informal conversations during which he learned from other ministers how churches function and how to deal with pastoral issues. The services of worship provided models for up-front leadership. Often, special conference leaders provided training on a wide variety of subjects.

Fourth, he participated in the district ministers meetings and congregational meetings. These meetings served as ministerial formation and accountability groups. Revivals and other special services in the district provided opportunities both for seeing how church was conducted in other places and for hearing guest preachers.

Fifth, he invited missionaries, Christian education leaders, evangelists, other pastors, guest musicians, college representatives, national agency leaders, as well as college singing groups to his churches. Most of the guests, other than groups, stayed in our home. (One outstanding occasion was the week when Raymond S. and Cleopatra Jackson, African Americans from Detroit, stayed in our southern Illinois home and led revival services in a town of 10,000 where only one person of color lived and where the unwritten law was that no other persons of color were to stay overnight. With the Jacksons, we had a week-long "intensive class," as we would call it at the seminary, in theology, hymnology, worship, church administration, the devotional life, intercultural relations, and social change.) I remember long and involved conversations with many, many church leaders at our table about all sorts of matters. Dad learned missionary theology, doctrine, principles of Christian education, stewardship, churchmanship, leadership skills, and interpersonal skills as these persons spent time with us, sometimes even longer than a week. This ongoing stream of persons significantly influenced us; they enriched not only Dad, but also the whole family, and helped to equip all of us for service.

Dad's experience, however, was not unique. I am confident that the description I have given of his process of being equipped for ordained ministry is reflective of literally thousands of faithful, effective, exemplary ministers in the Church of God. I praise God for them, both those who have gone on before us and those who continue to minister among us. I give this much space to my father because I honor the kind of ongoing equipping he and so many others represent.

However, we have witnessed many changes since the time when this kind of ministerial preparation and equipping was common. In many instances,

- The pastor's study is now merely the church office.

- Books have been replaced by television, seminars, conferences, tapes, and the Internet.

- Doctrinal journals have been replaced by informational, promotional, and inspirational publications.

- Camp meetings are no longer times for doctrinal and leadership formation but for recreation and fellowship.

- The percentage of pastors who attend camp meetings has greatly decreased.

- The percentage of pastors who attend district ministers meetings has decreased.

- Inter-congregational meetings are few and far between.

- Church guests stay in motels instead of the pastor's home.

I do not say this as though we should try to return to all of the former practices. Some of those practices have to do with irreversible social patterns. My purpose is to remind us of two matters: (1) In the past, we had informal ways for equipping ordained ministers, but (2) those informal opportunities for training are no longer in place.

Both before and during the era when my father was serving as a pastor, the church moved toward a more formal mode of ministerial preparation and equipping. First was the ministerial preparation that took place in connection with the missionary homes that were established in many cities around the country. According to Merle Strege, the official historian of the Church of God, eventually nearly fifty such homes were founded in small towns and large cities. Some functioned primarily as rescue missions and some as social aid centers, but all of them served as centers for Church of God life in those towns and cities. They were places where traveling revivalists and evangelists could stay, and where persons new to the movement could learn more about it, be formed spiritually and theologically by the Church of God, receive what Strege calls "rudimentary training" for ministry and where they could learn basic skills of administration. Some homes even developed more formalized courses of study.

Eventually, however, the missionary homes gave way to explicitly educational institutions. The Spokane Bible Institute (forerunner of Pacific Bible College and now Warner Pacific College) in Spokane, Washington, was begun in 1913. Anderson Bible Training School (forerunner of Anderson University) in Anderson, Indiana, was established in 1917. Warner Memorial University in Eastland, Texas, had its first classes in 1929. Alberta Bible College (forerunner of Gardner College) in Camrose, Alberta, Canada, was founded in 1932. South Texas Bible Institute (forerunner of Gulf-Coast Bible College, now Mid-America Christian University in Oklahoma City, Oklahoma) was launched in 1953, as was Arlington College in Southern California. In 1961, Bay Ridge Christian College was founded, and in 1968 Warner Southern College (now Warner University) held its first classes in Lake Wales, Florida. An important reason for the establishment of each of these institutions was the preparation and equipping of ordained ministers.

In addition, persons who had college degrees were pursuing further studies for the ordained ministry by enrolling in established seminaries, and some were pursuing doctoral studies. With this heightened interest in graduate-level studies, in 1950, Anderson College opened its own graduate level School of Theology for persons seeking graduate level education.

Another approach to ministry very different from the above has been with us from the very beginning of our history, and that is the assumption that no particular preparation is required. It is a straightforwardly anti-education stance. This stance is related to the theological perspective that the only requirements are for a person to have a sense of being called by God; give evidence of having a deep, personal spirituality; and exhibit evidence that one has spiritual gifts for ministry. That the church would require more than this is considered both inappropriate and arrogant. Being accepted as an ordained minister, then, is considered to be little more than group assent to an individual's personal experience of call, spirituality, and giftedness. It has little or nothing to do with the church's perspective as to what it needs in its ordained ministers for the edification of the church. The church's perspective is displaced by the individual's personal experience.

To summarize, we have at least four streams of ministerial preparation in the life of the church:

- Ministers who are *committed* to being equipped *informally* beyond a sense of divine call, personal spirituality, and giftedness for ministry.

- Ministers who are *committed* to being equipped *formally* beyond a sense of divine call, personal spirituality, and giftedness.

- Ministers who are *not* committed to being equipped beyond a sense of divine call, personal spirituality, and

giftedness. These are not committed to further preparation simply because they have not been challenged to
make such a commitment or because they perceive that
it is impossible, given the circumstances of their lives.

• Ministers who are overtly ***resistant*** **to being equipped**
beyond a sense of divine call, personal spirituality, and
giftedness.

We as a church need to do some serious grappling with this
whole issue. What should be our standard for the adequate preparation and equipping of our ordained ministers? In other words,
what should the church be able to count on in its ordained ministers? If the church sees the name of a person on a list of the
ordained, what should it be able to assume that means?

For instance, if I see a list of active airplane pilots, I should
be able to make certain assumptions about the persons on that
list without knowing each and every one of them. I assume that
every person on that list has the ability to see. I assume that each
person on the list knows how to get an airplane into the air. I assume that each and every person on the list knows how to guide
the airplane. I assume that every person knows what to do in case
of distress in flight. I assume that each person on the list knows
how to land an airplane. And I make many more assumptions.
I assume that those who have given those pilots their licenses to
fly have checked out all these things and more. Therefore, I as a
passenger do not have to check out the pilots of the planes on
which I fly.

Likewise, it seems to me that when a congregation sees the
name of someone listed as an ordained minister of the Church
of God, it should be able to assume the following is true without
knowing the individual personally. It should be able to assume
that the credentials committees have raised appropriate questions
in each of the following categories.

Personal, Christian faith.
Do they have a personal testimony of Christian faith? Have they been immersed in water baptism?

A sense of personal, divine call to ordained Christian ministry.
Is it on the basis of prayer that they have come to the conclusion that they are called to ordained ministry?

The call of the church to the ministry of the Word and worship.
Does the church closest to these persons recognize in them the call, the spirituality, the gifts, the knowledge, and the skills that are necessary for preaching and teaching the Word and for leading the people of God in experiences of worship?

Preparation in biblical studies.
Are they students of Scripture? Do they know more about Scripture than the average congregant does? Do they understand the Scriptures in their original context?

Are they able to exegete biblical texts? That is, are they able to read out of particular verses of Scripture what the text itself says?

Can they do expository work on all books of the Bible? That is, are they able to develop their own understanding of longer passages in harmony with the thought of the biblical author?

Can they do topical and doctrinal teaching and preaching? That is, are they able to identify themes in Scripture that help us deal with particular issues and doctrinal understandings, and in such a way that no violence is done to the biblical passages used? Are they able to present this exegetical, expositional, topical, and doctrinal work so that the Word comes alive in the present context? Is their preaching and teaching both informative of original biblical meanings and transformative of the way congregants live?

Knowledge of, appreciation for, and harmony with the biblical, historic Christian faith.
Do they know the defining line between historic Christian faith and aberrations of it? Do they know the importance of Trinitarian

thought in the life of the church? Are they themselves Trinitarian, and are they able to help the people of God with these matters? Do they know the importance of teaching the full divinity and the full humanity of Jesus Christ? Can they articulate clearly the biblical, historic understanding of the person and work of Jesus Christ? Are they personally committed to the historic understanding of the person and work of Christ? Are they informed about the history of the Christian church? Do they understand where the Church of God stands in relation to that long history?

Knowledge of, appreciation for, and harmony with the persistent historic perspectives and values of the Church of God.
Do they know the history of the Church of God reformation movement? Are they knowledgeable about the doctrinal understandings of the Church of God? Do they resonate with those historic understandings? Can they interpret those understandings? Are they committed to functioning within the context of those understandings and values?

Christian ethical and moral standards.
Is their ethical and moral life an open book to the ordination body? Do they exhibit practical holiness in all relationships? Are they living exemplary lives at the present time? Are they emotionally mature? Do they know and practice professional boundaries in relation to sexual matters? Has the ordination body scrutinized them carefully on these subjects? Have moral and ethical issues been duly addressed?

Ability to work with the people of God for the glory of God.
Do they have good relational skills? Do they have appropriate attitudes toward the people of God? Are they able to function as a participant within the covenant community of faith?

Skills that are necessary for the practice of ordained ministry.
Can they preach and/or teach the Word in an engaging way? Can they lead in public prayer? Can they lead in the Lord's Supper?

Can they function well in other special times of ministry such as baptisms and baby dedications? Can they lead people to Christ? Can they plan and lead a service of public worship? Can they make pastoral calls? Can they minister to people in times of special need? Do they have basic organizational and administrative skills? Do they have basic social skills that enable them to function without embarrassment in the public arena?

As we go through this list, most of us would say, "Yes, indeed, we do want ordained ministers who meet all of the above standards." How then do we go about developing a church environment in which our ordained ministers are in fact equipped in such a way? We are deeply indebted to the superb leadership of those who are working so diligently in credentialing, but we still have lots of work to do in terms of our grassroots understanding of what this is all about. And we need to address additional issues. Developing the kind of environment in which the equipping of our ordained ministers is a high priority requires work on the part of:

- Credentialing bodies.
- Educational institutions.
- Local congregations.
- Those who sense a call to ordained ministry.

It requires coordination so that we will have a unified approach to this issue, and so that ordination will have the same standard all across the board. It seems to me that it is time for all of us to unite in calling a halt to our patchwork approach. The idea of some ordained ministers being listed on the basis of one set of standards and others being listed on the basis of a very different set of standards leads to confusion, and inequity. In some cases, this prompts ministry candidates to cross district lines in order to get ordained more easily.

Persons come into ordained ministry at many different ages and with many different kinds of life experience. Both credentialing bodies and educational institutions need to take these differing factors into account. Obviously, the church in other parts of the world has to develop approaches that fit their respective circumstances. But in terms of the North American context, I would like to see all of our state and provincial credentials committees adopt standard tracks for preparation and equipping for ordained ministry. First of all, we need consistent standards for young people who sense a call to the ordained ministry. When a teenager in whatever state or province feels called, I would like for the church to present them with a plan as to how one goes about preparing and being equipped for such service. My experience is that young people like to be challenged. I think that many young people who otherwise would enter the Christian ministry go in another direction for at least one of seven reasons:

- We do not challenge them to consider the call.

- We do not nurture them once they have said yes to the call.

- We do not encourage and uphold such persons equally. We have too much discrimination, for instance, against females and against those who do not have the "right" racial characteristics.

- We do not adequately support them financially. I rejoice in the Blackwelder Funds made available for Church of God students at Anderson University School of Theology. That is an enormous help. And I rejoice at the scholarships that so many individuals have established. And yet, with all of these financial support systems, much more needs to be done.

- We do not give them a clear-cut plan for equipping themselves for the call.

- We do not hold a high enough preparation standard for them to reach.

- We do not insist that they follow the plan.

For instance, credentials committees could set forth the following straightforward **plan for all teenagers anticipating ordained ministry**:

1. Take advantage of the opportunities provided by the Leadership Development Task Force of Church of God Ministries. This informal support and nurturing process provides the setting for getting acquainted with other young people with the same calling and for dealing with questions and issues that emerge in the course of their early pilgrimage.
2. Invest yourself in church life, prayer life, and personal growth and development, and never quit. Having a deep, personal association with the church is basic to your spiritual formation for the ministry.
3. After high school graduation (at about age eighteen), get a broadly based college education at one of our endorsed church-related schools (Anderson University, Mid-America Christian University, Warner Pacific College, Warner University) or at an affiliated church-related school (Gardner College). This may include majoring in Christian ministries at these schools. The Church should be able to assume that all of her endorsed and affiliated schools are committed to the historic vision of the Church of God and that students will find an environment in which both their call to ordained ministry and their appreciation of the historic vision will be nurtured.
4. After college (at about age twenty-two), do the three-year Master of Divinity degree at Anderson University School of Theology (finishing at about age twenty-five). The Church should be able to assume that its seminary

173

is committed to the historic vision of the Church of God and that its curriculum addresses adequately all of the standards for ordination listed above in this chapter. If not Anderson, attend a seminary approved by the church which seminary includes in its curriculum the requirement to take courses in Church of God history, theology, and polity.

5. Pursue ordination after your formal educational process is finished. Too often we confuse the educational process and the ordination process. The two are certainly interrelated but they have different foci. The purpose of the educational process is to give students the opportunity to grow and develop, to ask questions and to grapple with big issues. The purpose of the ordination process is to assess whether the person is compatible with the church, and will minister beneficially within it. Education is about preparation and equipping. Ordination is about assessment and discernment. (After ordination, continuing education should be pursued for as long as one is in ministry.) Assuming that ordination takes place after initial preparation and equipping, it could take place at about age twenty-seven.

Following this track would place one at the point of ordination even three years younger than our Lord himself was when he entered his own public ministry!

A plan for traditional college-age persons who sense the call to ordained ministry while they are in college:

- Establish a mentoring relationship through the Leadership Task Force.

- Invest yourself in church life, prayer life, and personal growth and development, and never quit.

- After graduation from college, take the Master of Divinity degree at Anderson University School of Theology or at another seminary approved by the church which seminary requires for them courses in Church of God history, theology, and polity.

- Pursue ordination (which could take place at about age twenty-seven).

A plan for those who sense the call to ordained ministry after having been out of college no more than ten years (about age thirty-two):

- Establish a mentoring relationship through the Leadership Task Force.

- Invest oneself in church life, prayer life, and personal growth and development, and never quit.

- Take the Masters program in basic ministerial studies at Mid-America or at Warner Pacific, or the Master of Theological Studies at Anderson University School of Theology. The church should be able to assume that these programs are committed to the historic vision of the Church of God and that the curriculum adequately addresses all of the standards for the ordained ministry set forth above in this chapter. Graduation could take place at about age thirty-four.

- Pursue ordination which could take place at about age thirty-six.

A plan for persons later in life and with no college education:

- Establish a mentoring relationship with the state or provincial credentialing body.

- Invest oneself in church life, in prayer life, in personal growth and development, and never quit.

- Either major in Christian ministries at one of our Church of God undergraduate schools; or major in Christian ministries at a non–Church of God Christian college with transfer courses in Church of God history, theology, and polity; or take a non-degree course of study through the Center for Christian Leadership at Anderson University School of Theology. The church should be able to assume that in all of the schools mentioned, the curriculum adequately addresses all of the standards for ordination set forth above in this chapter.

- Pursue ordination after one's course work is finished.

Obviously, some in the last two categories will desire to pursue college and/or seminary. I presently have a seminary student who will be graduating this year at age fifty-seven.

I fully recognize that what I have set forth above goes against the grain for some of us. I also fully recognize the effective ministry of some among us who have never been on any of these educational tracks. In no sense do I disparage, begrudge, or berate their respective ministries. All of the evidence points to the fact that they are, indeed, equipped for ministry, even though they have not been on any of the formal educational tracks set forth above. I praise God for their ministries. I take pleasure in its fruitfulness. In no sense do I consider it to be inferior. They are well-prepared, well-equipped ministers in the life of the church. Hallelujah for the evidences of the Spirit's work in their lives and ministries, and Hallelujah that they have taken it upon themselves to equip themselves informally in the necessary biblical, historical, and theological knowledge, and in ministerial skills.

However, such persons are the exception rather than the rule. Most of us are not exceptional. I'm very much an example of the non-exceptional. I have needed and continue to need more structure than exceptional people need. It seems to me that we need to accept the fact that most of us are not in the exceptional category. Most of us need formal structures for preparation, formation, and equipping.

I know that preparation, formation, and equipping is much, much more than a matter of taking classes, passing tests, graduating from institutions, and accumulating certificates and diplomas. Too many who get degrees flunk out in the practice of ministry. I hope that I have adequately emphasized this in what I said above regarding the basic requirements for ordination, which include spirituality, call, giftedness, preparation in the Word, knowledge, Christian ethics, morality, relational health, and ministerial skills. So again I say: it is not a matter of either/or but both/and: both (1) divine call, personal spirituality, and giftedness and (2) being equipped in the Word, in historical and theological knowledge, Christian ethics, and in ministerial skills.

What will happen if we do not attend to this issue of equipping our ministers according to the broad range of matters discussed above? We already know what happens. In too many cases, we see the results when ministers lack adequate moral and spiritual formation; when they lack biblical, theological, and historical knowledge; when they lack basic ministerial skills. Some of the results are:

- Churches that have little or no theological and doctrinal commitment to the historic vision of the Church of God.

- Ordained ministers who do not know how to function in their professional lives.

- Congregations that are usurped by other Christian groups.

- Unnecessary confusion about congregational identity.

- Preaching that has lost its integrity.

- Ordained ministers and congregations that begin falling outside the circle of biblical, historic Christianity without even knowing it.

- Disorder in church life and in personal lives.

More could be said about this, but this has sufficiently sketched the dilemma in which we find ourselves. Thank God, this is not the case all across the board! But unless we do the very unpopular things I am calling for, I believe that the historic vision will be lost, and the Church of God reformation movement will dissipate.

While the emphasis in this chapter is on the ordained ministry, local congregations also have responsibility for the way they function. Both beneficial and dysfunctional ways exist for congregations to function. Issues having to do with congregational life will be addressed in the next three chapters.

CHAPTER 9

Requiring Accountability for the Sake of the Vision

Judges 17:6 says, "In those days there was no king in Israel; all the people did what was right in their own eyes." And the book ends at 21:25 with the same words. Israel hobbled along without any national accountability. All were doing their own thing.

After the morning service, the guest preacher was riding home with his host. They passed a Church of God near the host's house. "Is that one of our churches?" the guest preacher asked. "Yes," the host replied, "it's listed in the *Yearbook*, but they do their own thing. I've never even been in that church building. Our two congregations have nothing to do with each other."

He was guest speaker for a state meeting. Not far from that location, the nearest Church of God was having its own local gathering using another guest at the state meeting for its local purposes. Consequently, none of the ministerial staff of the nearby congregation appeared at the state meeting.

Her heart was broken. In anguish she told about the circumstances that had led to her congregation becoming theologically a very different church, especially in regards to matters of eternal security and the return of the Lord. She had nothing but praise for the pastoral skills of the ministers, but now in her elder years, after investing her life in the Church of God, she finds herself in an independent Baptist church. She had no problems with accepting as fellow Christians those with independent Baptist views, but that is not the kind of congregation she intended to be in. Because of the breakdown of accountability, that congregation is listed in the *Yearbook* but is theologically an independent Baptist church.

In a multistate meeting, many ministers were struggling with how they were to relate to the establishment of a competing organizational structure about which they had no voice. It sounded foreign to the way they think about being church. They were in anguish about how to handle this new reality about which they had not been consulted.

After serving as guest preacher in a local church and receiving words of appreciation for the quality of his preaching, he was taken by the pastor to the nearby camp meeting where he was to serve as evangelist. After the pastor got the evangelist settled in, he left and never returned. The evangelist learned that this was the pastor's standard practice, regardless of who the evangelist was.

A seminarian in his first church needed support from the larger churches in his area, but they were too busy to be involved. Their pastors were unavailable whenever he tried to connect with them.

A church called a man from another state to serve as their pastor without checking with anyone about his credentials. He had told them he felt a burden for their area of the country. Coming without his wife, they were under the mistaken impression that he was divorced. Once on the scene, though, he began dating a woman in the local church. After a while he took her with him to another state to candidate in yet another church. When the original church discovered what he had done, they fired him. This led to legal action and eventually to the obliteration of the congregation.

What price we pay for the lack of mutual accountability! "In those days there was no king in Israel; all the people did what was right in their own eyes."

Unless attention is given quickly to this matter, our church life together will come unraveled. This matter of accountability is related to the whole issue of being willing to work within the context of a covenant community. Covenant communities have specified ways of functioning. In order for them to work well, the participants in the covenant have to submit to the will of the community. This does not mean abandoning our responsibility to ask probing questions. It is not about becoming spiritual robots. Instead, it means:

- Deciding whether indeed we are called by God to be a covenant community.

- Coming to a mutual understanding about the requirements for living in covenant with each other.

- Developing the structures by which we go about being such a community.

- Practicing mutual accountability within those structures.

- Submitting our individual desires to the greater wisdom of the community.

No local congregation can function well unless these principles are followed. If everyone in a local congregation were to do what was right in their own eyes, it would be chaos. While most, if not all, of us recognize the importance of these principles on a congregational level, we jettison them when it comes to being a community of faith in a larger sense. Too often another set of values, perspectives, and modes of operation are followed. While on the local congregational level we know that everyone cannot do his or her own independent thing, on the intercongregational level we function in a very different way.

If I were speaking to one of our local congregations in chaos, I would ask:

- Do you agree among yourselves that God has a mission for you? If so, what is it? If not, why don't you disband?

- Do you have in place a preaching, teaching, and leadership ministry that is in theological harmony with the historic vision of the Church of God?

- If you know what your mission is, what do you believe is expected of everybody who is a member of this congregation? What should individuals expect from the congregation, and what should the congregation expect from individuals?

- Does the organizational structure of your church enable you to fulfill your mission? If not, are you willing to change it so that the mission can be fulfilled?

- Do you hold each other accountable within the context of your agreed upon covenantal agreement and organizational structure?

- What attitudes do you have about the importance of individuals functioning in ways that are compatible with the historic vision of the Church of God?

To the degree a congregation does not deal with these questions, it will be dysfunctional. Likewise, these are critical issues for the Church of God as a whole to seriously consider:

- Has God called us to be a distinctive fellowship of Christians? If so, to what has he called us, and are we committed to that mission? If not, why don't we disband?

- Do we have in place a leadership ministry that is in theological harmony with the historic vision of the Church of God?

- If God has called us to be a distinctive fellowship of Christians, what do we expect of each congregation, agency, and organizational structure within our fellowship? What do we expect of the ordained ministry?

- Do our organizational structures enable us to accomplish our mission? If not, are we willing to change them so that they will enable us to do so?

- Are we accountable to each other on the basis of our covenants and organizational structures? Are congregations accountable to anyone outside themselves? Are agencies and other organizational structures accountable to the church? Do they give a public report of all decisions and policies? Do they report the facts of their business affairs and programmatic decisions without any public relations spin? Is the biblical teaching about straightforward accuracy followed (i.e., the instruction in Matthew 5:37 to say "yes" only if we mean "yes" and to say "no" only if we mean "no")? Are ordained ministers and other officers and leaders of the church accountable to others within the fellowship?

- How well do we do with the spiritual discipline of submitting to the wisdom of the whole as long as it has nothing to do with doctrinal error, immorality, or ethical transgressions? Are we hobbling along with everyone doing what seems right in one's own eyes, or are we functioning as a covenant community of faith?

- Is it acceptable to ask questions at every level of church life as long as the questions are not meanspirited? Have we ruled out the notion that it is somehow unspiritual to ask honest questions in the spirit of love? Have we not had enough painful experiences at every level of church life because honest questions were not allowed, addressed straightforwardly, and openly discussed?

In connection with these questions, I would like to make three additional observations:

First, I believe we need to do an all-church inquiry, asking all of our congregations and ordained ministers whether they desire to explicitly declare themselves to be an active part of this distinctive fellowship of churches. The congregational decision about this should be made with full participation of the pastoral leadership, with full participation of the official corporate structure of the congregation, in accordance with the legal decision-making processes in the congregation, and with full information regarding legal safety clauses pertaining to property held by the church. Such a declaration would give us a sense of how much unity of purpose we have among us. For too long we have made assumptions that prove to be dysfunctional. We find ourselves playing games as though all of the congregations and ministers listed in the *Yearbook* were actually intentional about being committed to the historic vision of what we are about.

This dysfunctionality is illustrated by a pastor who said to newcomer that even though the congregation continues to be listed in the *Yearbook*, it no longer understands its identity in relation to the Church of God but in relation to another group. The fact that the congregation is listed in the *Yearbook* misrepresents the congregation as being committed to the historic vision of the Church of God.

Second, we need to develop covenants within the fellowship. The agencies of the national church are already required to do so. Why shouldn't every organizational component of the church—including local congregations and state and provincial organizations—do the same? A foundational issue in the covenant would have to do with whether the congregation (or other organizational structure) is in basic agreement with the historic vision of the church. Another issue would have to do with its responsibility to the whole church. What can the rest of us expect of it? To whom is it responsible? Is there any church body that can take the initiative to intervene when the congregation gets either into a self-destructive mode, or departs from the covenant, either in terms of the historic vision or in terms of immorality or ethical problems?

I am fully aware that the idea of bringing all congregations on board with this kind of covenant is unrealistic. However, such a policy could be established for church plants, and existing churches could be invited to consider entering a similar covenant. A statement like the one found in Appendix 4 could be included in the legal documents of such churches.

A student from another church fellowship came in to talk to me about his burden to be a church planter. He felt uncomfortable with some of the theological positions and practices of his denomination. My counsel to him was that it would be unethical for him to accept sponsorship from his denomination for a church plant not in harmony with the supporting denomination. They would assume that he intended to plant a church that was one of theirs. I suggested to him that he had three ethical options:

1. Review his disagreements to make sure whether they are matters of conscience. If, in fact, it turns out that they are matters of conscience, he would have to exit. If, however, they are not matters of conscience, then he has to ask himself whether he can submit to the collective wisdom of the denomination and proceed to plant a church that is to be both supported by them and identified with them.
2. If he does not want to plant a church that is to be identified with the denomination, he needs to tell his sponsors that and ask whether they are willing to support a church plant that is not harmonious with their historic perspectives and practices. If they are, then he can proceed with good conscience that he has been honest with them.
3. If he is not willing to plant a church that is harmonious with the denomination and is unwilling to tell them so, then he should seek his support elsewhere.

In a recent meeting with leaders of that denomination, I learned that plans for the church plant are moving along well with everything out in the open. All indications are that he has chosen to work within the framework of his covenant community.

This should be the way we function at every level of church life: within the framework of a covenant community.

My third observation is that we need to give attention to the ministry of oversight. This ministry should have the authority to intervene when matters get out of hand. We need to establish a ministry of collegial, consultative oversight. *Collegial* means that more than one person is involved (three, for instance) and that they are accountable to the body that placed them in that position. *Consultative* means that the overseers intervene only on the basis of consultation both with each other and with the congregational leadership. This ministry of collegial, consultative oversight, then, is to be distinguished from individualistic, dictatorial oversight.

Our church landscape is strewn with the wreckage of congregations destroyed by internal dysfunctionality. More often than not, people on the outside knew that the congregations were in a self-destructive mode, but all that anyone could do was to stand by and watch it happen. As a result, the investments that others made in the congregations are trashed, spiritual lives are endangered, and enormous emotional damage is suffered.

The ministry of oversight—even collegial, consultative oversight—can be misused. But so also can autonomous independency. Each carries its own baggage and possibilities of misuse. The two questions, however, that we need to deal with are the following.

Which is more biblical, the ministry of oversight or autonomous independency? And which of the two has the heavier baggage?

In answer to the first question, I believe that the New Testament church was not a collection of autonomous, independent churches but that it was a covenant community. What went on in local congregations was attended to not only by the persons within the local church but also by persons beyond the local congregation. In the New Testament, we see much evidence of mutual accountability, both among the churches and among individual ministries. We see examples in these New Testament references: the Jerusalem Conference of Acts 15, Paul's oversight of multiple churches, Paul's return to the church in Jerusalem (Acts 15; 18:22; 21:17–20) and to Antioch of Syria to give an account of his missionary travels (Acts 14:27–28; 18:22), and John's relation to the seven churches of Asia.

In my view, the answer to the second question is that our tendency during our more recent years to go the local autonomy, independency route has robbed us of our effectiveness. As a former pastor in New England, from time to time I am asked why we have so few churches there. Questioners often assume that it must be because New Englanders are resistant to a life-changing gospel. But that is not the case: both the Church of the Nazarene and the Assemblies of God have a strong witness throughout New

England. The difference between them and us is that they have a ministry of effective oversight and we do not. Is our practice of autonomous independency so precious that we are willing to hobble along for another century with a few churches—mostly small, struggling ones? Or are there other values we prefer to pursue in the years to come, namely, healthy, growing, dynamic churches where more people are being won to Christ and maturing in the faith? Personally, I prefer the baggage of a collegial, consultative ministry of oversight instead of the baggage of independency. I'm convinced that the former can be more helpful to the kingdom than the latter.

CHAPTER 10

Connecting Corporately for the Sake of the Vision

From the earliest days of the Church of God reformation movement a strong sense of being connected with each other has existed. We were in ministry together. We belonged to each other. We cared about what went on throughout the length and breadth of the movement. We were family. And to a great extent this still exists, but that historic sense of connectedness is eroding rapidly. I call it to our attention so that we can be intentional about what takes place next. Do we find it acceptable to lose this sense of connectedness? Are we comfortable with that loss?

The nature of our connectedness is different than in most church groups. Their connectedness is preserved by an organizational structure. When denominations are formed, working groups meet to decide on how they will be organized, how they will make decisions as a denomination, and how each congregation fits into the whole. These and many other decisions are made regarding belief, mission, polity, governance, and procedures. Once these matters are in place, those who are in agreement with the decisions give consent and the denomination is born. Younger denominations such as the Church of the Nazarene and the Assemblies of God can show pictures of the historic gatherings when their denominations officially came into existence. Although both of these denominations have seen lots of changes since their birth dates, they nevertheless have been connected by organizational structures that provide orderly ways for dealing with theological, doctrinal, polity, social, and other changes.

Ours is a very different kind of story. We came into existence as a doctrinal movement. No gathering was called to work out an organizational structure or to decide on polity and governance procedures. No pictures were taken of the founding of the movement. No denomination was formed. As a genuine movement, we simply found our way as we faced practical challenges. In the course of time, issues having to do with holding property, doing church work, good order in ordination procedure, organizing congregations for legal purposes, dealing with conflict, pooling our resources to do things local congregations could not do well on their own, and pursuing new challenges—all of these necessitated decisions about how we should go about doing the work of God, and accomplishing what we believe we are called to do. So our organizational structures have all emerged little by little. They have been developed in response to practical necessity. They did not appear as a result of a grand plan. That is why when one surveys the state and provincial section of the *Yearbook of the Church of God* one finds a broad array of organizational names. I illustrate this by listing the wide variety of organizational names used to refer essentially to the same kind of state and provincial organizations. In the following list, X stands for the name of some state or province:

- General Assembly of the Church of God in X
- X Ministerial Assembly of the Church of God
- X General Assembly of the Church of God
- X Association of the Church of God
- Church of God in X
- X Assembly of the Church of God
- Church of God X Conference
- X Church of God
- X Ministries of the Church of God
- X District of the Church of God
- X Churches of God
- X Ministers and Workers Conference of the Church of God

- ▫ X Church of God Association
- ▫ X Ministerial and Campground Association
- ▫ X General Assembly
- ▫ X Mission of the Church of God
- ▫ General Assembly and Ministerial Council of the Church of God in X
- ▫ Association of the Churches of God in X
- ▫ Fellowship of Churches of the Church of God
- ▫ X Presbytery of the Church of God
- ▫ Executive Council of the Church of God in X

This list reminds us that we came into existence as a movement and not as a denomination. If we had come into existence as a denomination, all of the state and provincial assemblies would be called the same thing. That would have been decided at the beginning. But not so with us. Our nomenclature has developed in piecemeal fashion in the course of our history, and even at this point in our history resistance still exists to standardized terminology, reminding us of the spirit of independence among us—and fragmentation. But more importantly, it points to the fact we have not had a unified organizational structure over the years to provide us with a sense of ongoing connectedness.

So, what has been the source of our ongoing connectedness, if not organizational structure? It has to do with matters of historic vision. From the beginning this historic vision was enunciated in the *Gospel Trumpet* (GT)—later *Vital Christianity* (VC), in the vigorous publication business of the Gospel Trumpet Company (later Warner Press), in our songs, in our camp meetings, and in our doctrinal preaching. These were the things that held us together. Later, it was enunciated through *Christian Brotherhood Hour* (now Christians Broadcasting Hope: *ViewPoint*), a graded Sunday school curriculum, church related schools of higher education, and common endeavors, ministries, and missionary efforts. These supported our life together; they were the components of our ongoing connectedness.

But this is a different day. *The Gospel Trumpet* and *Vital Christianity* are no longer published. Warner Press has a much reduced publication ministry. Our songs are unknown in many of our churches. While camp meetings serve very good purposes, more often than not those purposes do not include doctrinal formation. Congregational preaching hardly ever deals with the historic vision of the church. *ViewPoint* has a mission—a very good one—but the historic vision of the church is not the primary emphasis. Many of our churches do not use our Sunday school curriculum. Our schools have broadened their appeal so that they are becoming less identifiable as Church of God schools. Many of our churches have a lack of commitment to common endeavors, ministries, and missionary efforts.

I mention these things not for the purpose of lamentation but to identify the scope of our challenge. While we have new publications, programs, and endeavors, nothing has evoked the church-wide emotional loyalty that the above did in earlier years. Other church groups have gone through similar developments. To be sure, what we have experienced is not at all unique to us. The thing that is different for us is that, while other church groups have an organizational structure that provides them with an ongoing connectedness even while they go through changes that are similar to ours, we do not have a denominational structure.

I'm always amused when people say, "Well, whether we like it or not, we are a denomination." I wonder whether they know how a denomination works. If we are one of those things, we are a very funny-looking one. Most people from church groups that are genuine denominations are dumbfounded at how we do things, once they get close enough to observe how things really work. Actually, we are a loosely associated network of congregations and other organizations.

Let's use the metaphor of a tent to compare ourselves with denominations. A denominational tent is held up by the central pole of its organizational structure. (Of course, it is much more than that. It includes their history, theology, and ministry. But all that is part and parcel of an organizational structure.) Our tent, however, has not been held up by an organizational structure. On the contrary, it has been held up by Gospel Trumpet Company (Warner Press) publications, camp meetings, doctrinal preaching, CBH/broadcasts, Sunday school curriculum, schools of higher education, and other cooperative endeavors.

As we have already said, this traditional tent pole has been whittled down so that we now have a collapsed canvas. Every person, congregation, agency, and organization listed in the *Yearbook of the Church of God* is under the canvas, so to speak, but the central pole is not raised high enough for us to have a good strong tent.

What we have, then, is a canvas (which encompasses everybody and every organization listed in the *Yearbook*). Instead of having one central pole, multiple little poles are sticking up here and there. We have one canvas with many little tent poles. Many of our churches and ministers find their primary self-identity in relation to the little tent poles rather than in relation to the central tent pole.

Also, some of our ministers and churches are more emotionally and theologically related to tents outside our canvas than they are to the Church of God. While they continue being under the canvas (i.e., they are still listed in the *Yearbook*), their real identity is not in relation to any tent pole under the canvas but to a completely different tent. Being under the Church of God canvas is simply an incidental fact of history. The Church of God tent does not define who they are.

I do not wish to imply that all of the little tent poles under the canvas are bad. Some of them make very good little tents. Neither is this to say that all the tents outside our own canvas are bad; again, some of them are very commendable. I am not calling into question the importance of associational life beyond our canvas. Nor am I condemning all little tent associational life under our canvas. The point is that unless we have a strong central pole to serve as our rallying point, we no longer can function as a church fellowship with a unifying mission. Without that central pole we will continue the fragmentation that is already so much a part of our life together.

Do we find anything disturbing about this development. If not, then nothing needs to be attended to. The process that is already underway just needs to be allowed to progress at its own rapid pace.

If, however, we find this process disturbing, we need to ask why. Is it mere nostalgia? Is it simply because we happen to enjoy our life together and don't want to see it dissipating? If that is all it is, it is highly unlikely that anything we might do would be able to stop the process.

Or is it a matter of the biblical vision of what it means to be the one universal body of Christ, by the power of the Holy Spirit, in harmony with New Testament emphases? If that is why we do not want to see the tent in a state of collapse, then we should devote our energies to seeing that the central pole is once again raised.

But how does one raise the central pole. First of all, a denominational church structure is not the answer. By this I am talking about erecting a structure that people are asked to join. People join the United Methodist denomination, the Church of the Nazarene denomination, the Assemblies of God denomination. The Christian church does not need another denomination that people are asked to join. Most observers agree that we are in a truly post-denominational era. If we were to try our hand at constructing a denomination, we would be building something that is already crumbling before we start. We would cut the heart out of why we came into existence in the first place, in which case the only legitimate approach would be to completely repudiate our association with the Church of God reformation movement. The building of another denomination is not why we come into existence.

As I see it, the only way to raise the pole is for the leaders, preachers, and teachers of the Church of God to come face to face with the questions as to whether we are genuinely committed to the historic vision of what it means to be the church that is pleasing to God. Will we preach it, teach it, prepare ordained ministers for it, and be accountable to each other for its sake? The pole that has to be raised is a truth pole. It is only as the truth of this historic vision is lifted up, celebrated, and lived out that the pole will be raised. Apart from our being caught up in the vision—committed to it, empowered to preach and teach and write about it, invigorated to spread the good word about it, and devoted to living it out in all dimensions of our church life—no pole will be lifted up. Apart from this, the fragmentation will proceed unabated. Apart from this, we will be little more than a footnote in the history of the Christian church.

Our ongoing connectedness has to be more than an organizational connectedness. It has to be a visionary connectedness. It has to be a truth connectedness. It has to be a relational connectedness. It has to be a celebrative connectedness. It has to be the connectedness made possible by an ordained ministry that is committed to and equipped for preaching and teaching this vision. It is a connectedness made possible by congregations and agencies and organizational structures that are accountable for what they do with the historic vision.

But what about all of the persons who are members of local congregations? Must all agree with the historic vision before becoming participants in the local congregation? The clear answer is No because according to Scripture, salvation is the basis for membership in God's one universal church, not agreement on all the details regarding the historic vision. Our first priority is to win people to Christ. Persons who come to Christ are thereby incorporated into Christ's one and only church. No one should ever ask new converts to join the Church of God reformation movement. Salvation is the critical matter. That salvation makes us all members of the one universal body of Christ is basic. However, as persons are nurtured in local congregations of the Church of God, the nature of that nurture should be according to the historic vision of what it means for a local congregation to be an expression of the one universal church, by the power of the Holy Spirit, in harmony with New Testament emphases. And in the course of time, we can hope that the truth will be taught, preached, and lived out so well that all will come to affirm that vision, be devoted to it, and live accordingly. We desire that everyone "see the church," as we used to say. But that must never be confused with being redeemed by the blood of the Lamb. "Seeing the church" is a doctrinal issue. Being redeemed is a salvation issue. It is important always to maintain this distinction.

Furthermore, we can affirm the participation of Christians in the life of congregations of the Church of God who do not agree with the historic understandings of the Church of God. No requirement should ever be made that all in our local congregations must agree with all of the historic understandings of the Church of God. People are not being asked to join a denomination. All should be welcomed into the fellowship of the one universal church. This does not mean, however, that our preaching, teaching, and leadership ministries should play down anything with which some do not agree. Going down that road is certain disaster. It is important for all who participate in the life of the church to know we have indeed come to some theological and doctrinal conclusions on a whole range of issues. All who are members of our congregations should be exposed to these particular doctrinal understandings of the Church of God, about which no apology is made. Whatever persons do with it, our responsibility is to faithfully preach, teach, and practice the historic vision, and to trust the Holy Spirit to do the rest.

CHAPTER 11

Living Out the Vision

I had just finished presenting the historic vision of the Church of God to an ecumenical gathering made up of a wide spectrum of Christian traditions. From the looks on the faces of those listening to me, I sensed great appreciation for what I had said and was ready to entertain questions that would give me additional opportunity to expand on the vision that I take delight in introducing to others.

The first to speak, however, did not have a question but a comment. He said, "What you have shared with us is very commendable and I personally find it to be a beautiful vision. However, as I listened to you I found it difficult to put it together with one of your congregations not far from where I minister. The people in that church are rigid, resistant to any association with the rest of us, and rude when we try to make contact with them. The general consensus in our town is that the people in that church simply do not want to have anything to do with the rest of us. They are quite happy doing their own thing. So, we leave them alone."

I did not have much juice left in me after he finished.

That painful experience leads me in this chapter to deal with some very practical matters. Our vision is powerless to affect others if it is not lived out in our local communities. Actions speak louder than words. As James 2:18 puts it: "I by my works will show you my faith." I, therefore, give the following guidelines for living out what it means to be an expression of the one universal church, by the power of the Holy Spirit, in harmony with New Testament emphases.

First of all, we should understand our local gatherings, and more particularly our services of worship, to be a foretaste of the heavenly assembly described in Revelation 7:9–10:

> After this I looked, and there was a great multitude that no one could count, from every nation, from all tribes and peoples and languages, standing before the throne and before the Lamb, robed in white, with palm branches in their hands. They cried out in a loud voice, saying, "Salvation belongs to our God who is seated on the throne, and to the Lamb!"

We notice in this passage that the heavenly assembly has at least the following characteristics.

- It consists of the whole spectrum of the human family.

- It is God-centered.

- It focuses on salvation through Christ.

- It is a celebrative fellowship.

To the degree that the gatherings in our congregations are a foretaste of the heavenly assembly, they will exhibit these same characteristics. They will be inclusive of all kinds of people. They will be God-centered and not us-centered. They will be salvation fellowships and not religious social clubs. They will be gatherings of Christian joy and not of legalistic religiosity.

Second, since we are called to be an expression of the one universal church, each congregation should have an open-door policy. That means that people of any race, any cultural background, any social standing are to be warmly welcomed into the fellowship of the church.

But each congregation should be more than simply accepting of whoever shows up. They need to be more actively involved in creating such diversity. Therefore, **third**, each congregation should be overtly intentional about broadening its constituency to reflect the fact that the one universal church is multiethnic, multiracial, and multicultural.

Fourth, at every level of our church life we should develop the skills of Christian hospitality. We are called to be the one universal body of the Christ who says in Matthew 11:28–30:

> Come to me, all you that are carrying heavy burdens, and I will give you rest. Take my yoke upon you, and learn from me; for I am gentle and humble in heart, and you will find rest for your souls. For my yoke is easy, and my burden is light.

In every dimension of our church life, we need to reflect this invitation of our Lord. I believe that it is important for us to make this as practical as possible because it is in the simple matters of church life that we do some of the greatest harm to the message we proclaim. I am thinking of how we function at church meals, welcome strangers, relate to each other in our church narthexes or public gathering places, answer the telephone, treat our church-building neighbors, and connect to other Christians.

Increasingly, I am convinced that Christians do not automatically have the skills for putting into action what we preach and teach. These skills have to be taught.

Have you ever been to **church potluck suppers** in which little friendship groups always sit together, seemingly oblivious to newcomers, outsiders, and the lonely persons in their midst? They seem to be unaware that the purpose of church meals is much more than simply providing space for their little groups to do what they could do in their own backyards or family rooms. As Paul said regarding a similar situation in the Corinthian church, "Do you not have homes to eat and drink in?" (1 Corinthians 11:22). The purpose of church meals is:

- To strengthen the relationships of the whole fellowship.
- To reach out to others.

▫   To incorporate those who attend into the welcoming arms of the fellowship of Christ.

I have been at church meals where no sense of community whatsoever was evident; it was simply a collection of little private groups. I have been at meals where single people, couples, and families were ignored by the rest of the diners and left to eat by themselves. The question is why they are left to eat alone in a space often called a *fellowship* hall. If they are going to eat alone anyhow, why not do it at the local McDonalds?

Do we know **how to welcome strangers**? What do we say to them? What basic information might the stranger need to know? How can we make the stranger feel comfortable in our space? An exercise that I suggest from time to time is for persons to go to a church where they are complete strangers, and see how it feels. What happened that made them feel comfortable? What happened that made them feel ill at ease? If a whole group of people in a local church were to do this in the same general frame of time, they could bring their multiple experiences back for discussion and reflection as to how their own local church does in this respect.

Now a word about **how we function in our narthexes** or public gathering places, before and after services: What goes on there is a test of the quality of church life. While the narthex may be a dynamic place of conversation, with many little groups enjoying each other's company, for others it may be a place of desolation. Such people may find it hard to break into social settings because of shyness, or they may be new in the congregation or first time visitors.

I once heard of a congregation that practiced in their narthex what they called the "horseshoe discipline." Any conversation group was always in the shape of a horseshoe so that others could easily join it or be invited into it.

We need to learn to lift up our eyes beyond the circle of our closest friends and find the lonely ones, the newcomers, and the shy ones. In the power of the Holy Spirit, we need to connect with them. We need lots of Pentecostal power in our narthexes.

I'm talking about what happened on the day of Pentecost when the church was empowered by the Holy Spirit to connect with strangers from all over the world. We need Pentecostal narthexes.

Your congregation might do well to invite an outside observer to analyze the dynamics of its narthex and report it to the church for discussion and any called-for action.

Answering the telephone is one of the most important tasks in the church. How that is done gives the caller his or her first impression about the church. A pleasant voice indicates that the church has a pleasant voice. Being helpful indicates that the church is helpful. Being professional indicates that the church is convinced that its work is very important. Graciousness in the conversation indicates that the church is a place of grace. Who answers the phone and how they do it should be a major consideration for any church regardless of its size, and for any church agency regardless of its function. No church-related phone is simply a business phone; it's a kingdom phone.

How we treat our church neighbors is critical to the effectiveness of our mission. I remember receiving a call from a church neighbor to our small congregation in Malden, Massachusetts. She was upset because we had developed the bad habit of putting our trash on the curb on Saturday for Monday pick-up. That made sense to us because that's when we cleaned the church building. But the neighbors didn't appreciate having to look at our trash all day Sunday. They were right. We apologized and began putting it out after the Sunday evening service. Some of the neighbors were so impressed that they began attending our services.

Keeping the property up, making proper provisions for parking, being sensitive to noise and lighting and signage issues—all these and more are good neighbor matters.

Also, **how we connect to other Christians** speaks loudly about who we are. I know of Church of God congregations that have a prayer ministry for non-Church of God congregations in their respective communities. They call the pastors of those congregations and ask for their requests for prayer. They then pray for those needs publicly. As a result, some personal friendships have been formed between the Church of God and some fiercely independent churches, for example, and with some churches with which it has major theological differences. The climate among Christians has been transformed in those communities as a result of that kind of prayer ministry.

Let us summarize how we live out the vision of being the kind of church that pleases God:

- We live out the vision by being a fellowship that is welcoming, hospitable, gracious, and caring.

- We live it out by being intentionally inclusive of people "from every nation, from all tribes and peoples and languages."

- We live it out by being glad bearers of the gospel in all that we say and do.

- We live it out by taking the study of Scripture seriously.

- We live it out by showing by the quality of our lives that the Lord has made us new creatures who bear the fruit of the Spirit.

- We live it out by our sacrificial and wholehearted service to the Lord.

- We live it out by "making every effort to maintain the unity of the Spirit in the bond of peace."

- We live it out by exhibiting "righteousness and peace and joy in the Holy Spirit."

- We live it out by our eagerness to share the gospel with the whole world.

CHAPTER 12

Sharing the Vision

If we are convinced that our historic vision is biblical and contributes to the well-being of the whole church of Jesus Christ, then we ought to use every means possible for sharing the vision. Instead of hoping that people will come to us, we need to take the initiative to go beyond our comfort zones and enter into those associations where we can be engaged with others.

Every local community has established associations of churches, such as holiness associations, evangelical associations, ministerial associations, women's groups, and councils of churches. States and provinces have organizations for cooperative work and mutual understanding. For example, Indiana Ministries of the Church of God belongs to a statewide organization called Indiana Partners for Christian Unity and Mission, which includes churches ranging across the spectrum of Pentecostal, Holiness, Evangelical, other Protestants, Roman Catholic, and Orthodox. On a national and international level several established venues for sharing our historic vision exists, including organizations in the United States like the National Association of Evangelicals and the National Council of Churches of Christ in the USA. Canada has comparable organizations. In the North American context venues include the just recently established U.S.-Canadian Foundation for a Conference on Faith and Order in North America, and on the world level organizations like the World Council of Churches.

Some among us are quite comfortable with one or more of these but uncomfortable with others. Some among us are comfortable with all of them. And some are uncomfortable with all.

It is possible, however, to relate to any and all of the above without compromising who we are, and in some cases to do so without actually joining the organizations as a church group. It is my experience that in each and every case, the door of welcome is open for conversation and sharing.

Some objections to taking advantage of such opportunities are the following.

Objection: We will compromise who we are if we get into these entangling alliances.

Response: That depends on whether we are in touch with who we are and are maturely self-confident. There is a difference between mature self-confidence and immature cockiness. Mature self-confidence enables a group to be engaged with others without losing touch with its own identity. Fear of losing our identity is born of theological insecurity. Such insecurity expresses itself either by self-exalting bravado as we interact with others, or by insulating ourselves from others.

Objection: Some of these groups are out to create a monolithic super church with the least common denominator as the basis.

Response: More than ever before, Christians at all levels believe that a monolithic superchurch is neither a possibility nor desirable. Christians in general are more than ever sensitive to the fact that different contexts call for different modes of operation. In general, Christian leaders are increasingly appreciative of the rich texture of the Christian faith that blesses us all. Trying to reduce Christian thought to as little as possible may be what a few ecclesiastical officials and theologians have aimed at from time to time, but most contemporary church leaders are certainly not in that mode of thought. They continue to keep the full range of theological issues on the table. In my experience of theological discussions in these settings, I am impressed with how devoted Christian leaders are to the full spectrum of Christian beliefs and how strongly they resist any effort to discount that full spectrum. That is why such discussions continue for decades. They have so much to discuss that understanding can't be developed in a short period of time.

Objection: Participation in such organizations is a waste of time. **Response:** It is true that some organizations are dysfunctional; some don't have a clear vision as to what they are about; some are worn out and need to die. However, that being said, many of these organizational structures provide golden opportunities for us to share an historic vision that we are convinced is a biblical vision of the church, and to develop a broader picture and better understanding of the church in our day. It is never a waste of time when we are talking with others about the biblical vision of the church.

I have some suggested guidelines for your involvement in such associations, whether local, state or provincial, national, or international:

1. Practice Christian graciousness in the relationship. The fruit of the Spirit count here, too.
2. Establish personal friendships with all who are open to such relationships.
3. Listen well to others.
4. Keep in mind that the above three items are necessary in order to earn the right to speak.
5. It is always important for us to be ourselves, and to represent our church heritage as honestly as we can.
6. Share with others the riches of our tradition of biblical faith, but also be willing to receive from others.
7. Always be up front with your constituency about your participation in any and every organization. Nothing should ever be on the sly.
8. Expect those outside our tradition to see things in us that we do not see. Sometimes they see oddities and weaknesses; sometimes they see jewels and strengths. We need the eyes of outsiders in order to see ourselves more accurately.

Also, outsiders often ask questions that we never think of asking ourselves. They help to sharpen both our theology and practice of the faith.

9. If we take such conversations seriously, we will earn the opportunity to do the same in relation to other Christians. We can help them to see in their theology and practice issues to which they are perhaps blind.

If the historic vision we have is truly of the Lord, as I am convinced it is, we are under divine obligation to take advantage of every opportunity to share it. We are to share it humbly, confidently, graciously, and prayerfully, all the while trusting the Lord of the church to use our faithful witness as he sees fit for the well-being of his whole church. Let us be who we are called to be, take every opportunity to share our historic vision, and leave the rest in the Lord's hands.

CONCLUSION

I was riding along with a longtime friend as he showed me the sights of his small city. He is a professional in one of the major institutions of the town. He knows the leaders of the community, and over the years has immersed himself in civic, cultural, and church life. He is a prominent member of one of the six local congregations of the Church of God, none of which has an average Sunday morning attendance of more than 130. "What role does the Church of God play in the religious life of this community?" I asked him. He thought for a long time before giving his answer: "We are incidental to church life in this community."

Before the word *incidental* escaped my memory, I wrote it down on a little paper bag I had in my hand, and I have not thrown it away yet. For something to be incidental means that it is secondary to the main thing. For instance, the color of the tie I wear when I go to Sunday worship at my local church is incidental to the event itself. The event is not at all about the color of the tie I wear. The event is about a congregation's worship of God. After the service is over, and a passerby asks someone coming out of the church what had drawn people there that day, the respondent is going to say something like, "We have been in worship." The person will not say, "We came to see Gil Stafford's tie," because that is merely incidental to the main event.

For us to be incidental in a community means that when an outsider asks someone about the religious life of the community, we figure into the description no more than the color of my tie fits into the description of why people gather on Sunday morning in my local church.

To what extent are we incidental to the religious life of our communities? In local settings, the answer will vary from place to place. But are we incidental to the church world as a whole? Are

207

we incidental in church history textbooks? Are we incidental in the thought life of the Christian church?

I do not believe that God has called us to be incidental. On the contrary, we are called to impact our communities, to impact the whole Christian church, to impact the world. But how do we go about impacting them? Do we do it by making so much noise that others have to give attention to us? Do we do it by making a nuisance of ourselves? Do we do it by making a big splash either in the media or with our buildings? Do we do it by having our people in positions of public visibility and power? Do we do it by having more people associated with us than others have associated with them? No, I pray God that we do not focus on any of these things.

My prayer is that we will impact our world by being and doing the following:

- By being Spirit empowered disciples who are making disciples both at home and abroad.

- By being good stewards of the historic vision of what it means to be an expression of the universal church, in harmony with New Testament emphases.

- By disciplining ourselves to live out this vision in every venue of our church life, whether locally, nationally or internationally.

- By being a confident, humble presence in every place God affords us the opportunity to be.

- By being lovingly engaged with the church world in whatever form we find it.

- By being the continuously refreshed and always refreshing people of God—that is, by allowing the feet washing Jesus to cleanse and refresh us for the journey of faith, and by committing ourselves to washing each other's feet so that all who associate with us will experience cleansing and refreshment for the journey.

- By being so well-grounded in the truth of Scripture that we are able to enter helpfully into theological and doctrinal discussions at every level.

- By being the community of the kingdom—that is, by living together in such a way that we are reflective of kingdom values.

- By being heralds of the kingdom—that is, our message is clearly the good news about the reign and rule of God: his reign and rule over the world, over the church, and in our hearts.

- By being sites where signs of the kingdom occur—that is, where miracles of physical healing, emotional healing, relational healing, spiritual healing, and social healing take place in our midst.

To be this kind of people is never to be incidental. We are never incidental when we are Spirit empowered disciples making disciples. We are never incidental when we take seriously what it means to live out the ramifications of being an expression of the universal church, in harmony with New Testament emphases. We are never incidental when we are confidently, humbly, and lovingly engaged with others outside our circle. We are never incidental when people always find refreshment in our midst. We are never incidental when we are biblically informed conversation partners. We are never incidental when we are truly a community of the kingdom. To live this way is to make a gobal impact that is pleasing to the Lord.

May it be so, O Lord! May it be so!

As Christians, Here We Stand

Editor's Note:

This revision is based on responses to the presentation of the original in meetings around the world. These included an open meeting, consisting of several hundred persons representing a cross-section of the church, at the North American Convention of the Church of God, in Anderson, Indiana, on June 21, 2000, and also several meetings in the United States to which I was invited to lead Crossroads conferences: Northern California; Florida; North Carolina; the Fort Wayne area in Indiana; Michigan (including Ontario, Canada); Alaska; Kansas; Central Michigan; Eastern States including Massachusetts, Rhode Island, Vermont, New York, Pennsylvania, Maryland, and New Jersey; and Colorado. Also, all career missionaries of the Church of God were asked to consult with leaders in their respective areas about the Confession. Written responses were received from church leaders in Bolivia, Costa Rica, Barbados, Tanzania, Rwanda, Kenya, Uganda, and Zambia. Other written responses were received from leaders in Yugoslavia, Russia, and Spain. Consultations with leaders in special Crossroads conferences took place also in these settings: the Japanese Pastors Conference, February 19–21, 2001; the Asian Leaders Conference in Hong Kong, March 5–9, 2001, which included leaders from India, Nepal, Cambodia, Myanmar, Australia, Philippines, Thailand, and China; Heads of Church of God Schools meeting in Fritzlar, Germany, March 15–18, 2001; the German Pastors Conference including leaders from Switzerland, the Netherlands, Bulgaria, and Russia), May 7–9, 2001; the Theological Conference in Western Canada, May 15–17, 2001; and a Crossroads Conference in Eastern Canada October 19–20, 2001.

Other consultations were held with leaders in Italy, Greece, and Hungary. In addition, at the 2001 North American Convention of the Church of God, another Crossroads Conference, open to everyone, was held during the whole afternoon of Sunday, June 17. In all of these conferences either the original Confession or the emerging "As Christians, Here We Stand" was read and discussed. Where English was not the first language the document was translated. Changes and additions were made in light of this international conversation. It is with confidence that I present it not simply as my personal understanding of the church's faith, but as the church's own understanding of its faith.

Introduction

We believe "all scripture is inspired by God and is useful for teaching, for reproof, for correction, and for training in righteousness, so that everyone who belongs to God may be proficient, equipped for every good work" (2 Timothy 2:16–17). We are nourished by "the sacred writings" that are able to instruct us "for salvation through faith in Christ Jesus" (3:15).[1]

We believe all the Bible teaches in light of the eternal Word incarnated in Jesus Christ. "In the beginning was the Word, and the Word was with God, and the Word was God" (John 1:1). "In him was life, and the life was the light for all people" (1:4). "And the Word became flesh and lived among us, and we have seen His glory," a glory that is "full of grace and truth" (1:14).

We are humbled by the vastness of God's revelation in the Bible. Although we recognize that we can never put into a short document all that we are taught in the Bible, we, nevertheless, believe it to be beneficial to confess at least some major themes of our faith, using the words of Scripture.

---

1. Emphasis has been added with the use of bold type to some words in the scripture quotations in order to provide a guide for the subject matter covered.

I. Confessions about God

In agreement with the historical Christian church's understanding of biblical faith, we believe in **the one eternally triune** God: Father, Son, and Holy Spirit (Matt 28:19).

Along with the ancient people of Israel, and with Jesus (Matthew 22:37), we confess, "**the LORD our God is one LORD**. You shall love the LORD your God with all your heart, and with all your soul, and with all your might" (Deut 6:4–5).

In harmony with a New Testament hymn of faith, we confess **Jesus Christ** as "the image of the invisible God, the firstborn of all creation; for in him all things in heaven and on earth were created, things visible and invisible, whether thrones or dominions or rulers or powers—all things have been created through him and for him. He himself is before all things, and in him all things hold together. He is head of the body, the church; he is the beginning, the firstborn from the dead, so that he might come to have first place in everything. For **in him all the fullness of God was pleased to dwell** and through him God was pleased to reconcile to himself all things, whether on earth or in heaven, by making peace through the blood of his cross" (Col 1:15–20).

Likewise, with Scripture, we confess that our Lord, in whom "all the fullness of God was pleased to dwell," was also **fully human**: "And being found in human form, he humbled himself and became obedient to the point of death—even death on a cross" (Phil 2:7d–8). And we believe he "died for our sins in accordance with the scriptures, and that he was buried, and that he was raised on the third day" (1 Cor 15:3–4).

In agreement with the New Testament, we confess, "Jesus is Lord" (1 Cor 12:3).

As people of resurrection faith, we experience "**the immeasurable greatness of his power** for us who believe, according to the working of his great power. God put this power to work in Christ when he raised him from the dead and seated him at his right hand in the heavenly places, far above all rule and authority and power and dominion, and above every name that is named, not only in this age but also in the age to come. And he has put all things under his feet and has made him the head over all things for the church, which is his body, the fullness of him who fills all in all" (Eph 1:19–23).

We rejoice at the outpouring of **the Holy Spirit** on the day of Pentecost, and experience the fulfillment of our Lord's promise when he said the "Advocate, the Holy Spirit, whom the Father will send in my name, will teach you everything, and remind you of all that I have said to you"(John 14:26). Thanks be to God!

II. Confessions about Salvation

We know that "all have sinned and fall short of the glory of God" (Rom 3:23), and recognize Jesus Christ as our only means of salvation. "There is **salvation** in no one else, for there is no other name under heaven given among mortals by which we must be saved" (Acts 4:12). Our Lord says: "I am the way, and the truth and the life. No one comes to the Father except through me" (John 14:6).

With the New Testament, we teach that the experience of this salvation requires both **personal repentance of sin and personal faith** in Jesus Christ. We know that "godly grief produces repentance that leads to salvation" (2 Cor 7:10), and we gladly proclaim, "God so loved the world that he gave his only Son, so that everyone who believes in him may not perish but may have eternal life" (John 3:16). We are convinced that "if anyone is in Christ, there is a new creation: everything old has passed away; see, everything has become new!" (2 Cor 5:17). We teach that the fruit of this new creation is "love, joy, peace, patience, kindness, generosity, faithfulness, gentleness, and self-control" (Gal 5:22).

And so, by divine grace working through personal repentance and faith, we have been buried with Christ "by **baptism** into death, so that, just as Christ was raised from death by the glory of the Father, we too might walk in newness of life" (Rom 6:4). In connection with this spiritual baptism, we preach and practice the immersion of believers, about which it is reported that on the day of Pentecost those who believed the gospel "were baptized, and that day about three thousand persons were added" (Acts 2:41).

But after baptism, as the pilgrim people of God, we are to "**press on** toward the goal for the prize of the heavenly call of God in Christ Jesus" (Phil 3:14).

As Christians, we are admonished to "be filled with the Spirit" (Eph 5:18), and "to lead a life worthy of the calling to which you have been called, with all humility and gentleness, with patience, bearing with one another in love, making every effort to maintain the unity of the Spirit in the bond of peace" (Eph 4:1–3).

As believers, we are instructed by these words: "My little children, I am writing these things to you so **that you may not sin**. But if anyone does sin, we have an advocate with the Father, Jesus Christ the righteous; and he is the atoning sacrifice for our sins, and not for ours only but also for the sins of the whole world" (1 John 2:1–2).

We know that as believers we are urged to present our "**bodies as a living sacrifice**, holy and acceptable to God," which is our "spiritual worship" (Rom 12:1). We take with seriousness the practical implications of these questions: "Do you not know that your body is a temple of the Holy Spirit within you, which you have from God, and that you are not your own? For you were bought with a price; therefore glorify God in your body" (1 Cor 6:19–20). And we believe that the following benediction is to be experienced in this life prior to death: "May the God of peace himself **sanctify you entirely**; and may your spirit and soul and body be kept sound and blameless at the coming of our Lord Jesus Christ. The one who calls you is faithful, and he will do this" (1 Thess 5:23–24).

We are convinced that God's sanctifying grace produces wholehearted love of both God and others: "Love has been perfected among us in this: that we may have boldness on the day of judgment, because as he is, so are we in this world. There is no fear in love, but **perfect love** casts out fear; for fear has to do with punishment, and whoever fears has not reached perfection in love. We love because he first loved us. Those who say, 'I love God,' and hate their brothers or sisters, are liars; for those who do not love a brother or sister whom they have seen, cannot love God whom they have not seen. The commandment we have from him is this: those who love God must love their brothers and sisters also" (1 John 4:17–21).

We believe that we are secure in **our salvation** so long as we remain faithful to Christ. As the faithful people of God, we take comfort in the promise of our Lord, "No one will snatch them out of my hand" (John 10:28). We are instructed, however, of **the necessity of continuing to abide in Christ** and are warned, "whoever does not abide in me is thrown away like a branch and withers; such branches are gathered, thrown into the fire, and burned" (John 15:6). "The one who endures to the end will be saved" (Matt 10:22). "But thanks be to God, who gives us the victory through our Lord Jesus Christ" (1 Cor 15: 57).

III. Confession about the Church

As followers of Jesus Christ, we accept his commission to "make disciples of all nations, baptizing them in the name of the Father and of the Son and the Holy Spirit, and teaching them to obey everything that I have commanded you" (Matt 28:19–20).

We affirm in the words of Scripture that "there is **one body** and one Spirit, just as you were called to the one hope of your calling, one Lord, one faith, one baptism, one God and Father of all, who is above all and through all and in all. But each of us was given grace according to the measure of Christ's gift" (Eph 4:4–7). This grace at work within us manifests itself always and without exception "so that the church may be built up" (1 Corinthians 14:5). We are guided by the truth that "there are **varieties of gifts**, but the same Spirit; and there are varieties of services, but the same Lord; and there are varieties of activities, but it is the same God who activates all of them in everyone. To each is given the manifestation of the Spirit for the common good" (1 Cor 12:4–7).

In humility, we understand ourselves to be a continuing fellowship of what the New Testament calls "**the church of God** that he obtained with the blood of his own Son" (Acts 20:28). We are convinced that the only way into this one, universal church of God is as Scripture reports: "the Lord added to their number those who were being saved" (Acts 2:47). We understand ourselves according to the proclamation: "But you are a chosen race, a royal priesthood, a holy nation, God's own people, in order that you may proclaim the mighty acts of him who called you out of darkness into his marvelous light" (1 Pet 2:9). On the day of Pentecost, the church was **empowered to be Christ's witnesses** "in Jerusalem, in all Judea and Samaria, and to the ends of the earth" (Acts 1:8). That empowerment took place as **the Spirit was poured out on people indiscriminately** so that "your sons and daughters shall prophesy, and your young men shall see visions, and your old men shall dream dreams. Even upon my slaves, both men and women, in those days I will pour out my Spirit; and they shall prophesy" (Acts 2:17–18).

Even as the seven churches of Asia were called to mend their ways, even so God continues calling his church to **reformation**. The following words addressed to all of the seven churches are addressed also to us: "Let anyone who has an ear listen to what the Spirit is saying to the churches" (Rev 2:7, 11, 17, 29; 3:6, 13, 22).

In accordance with the guidelines of Scripture, we take delight in **the fellowship of God's church**, "not neglecting to meet together, as is the habit of some, but encouraging one another," and all the more, as we "see the Day approaching" (Heb 10:25).

In historical continuity with the people of God, we are committed to corporate **worship** in accordance with the words of our Lord: "God is spirit, and those who worship him must worship in spirit and truth" (John 4:24). We gather to hear the **Scriptures read, preached, and taught**, for we remember that our Lord on the day of his resurrection did so: "Then beginning with Moses and all the prophets, he interpreted to them the things about himself in all the scriptures" (Luke 24:27). **We give of our resources** for the cause of Christ, knowing that "the one who sows sparingly will also reap sparingly, and the one who sows bountifully will also reap bountifully" (2 Cor 9:6). We lift up the ancient standard for our giving: "Bring the full tithe into the storehouse, so that there may be food in my house, and thus put me to the test, says the Lord of hosts; see if I will not open the windows of heaven for you and pour down for you an overflowing blessing" (Mal 3:10). We enjoy **singing** "psalms, hymns and spiritual songs … making melody to the Lord in our hearts" (Eph 5:19). We are committed to **prayer**, remembering the sacred instruction, "Do not worry about anything, but in everything by prayer and supplication with thanksgiving let your requests be made known to God" (Phil 4:6).

We **anoint "with oil in the name of the Lord"** and believe that "the prayer of faith will save the sick, and the Lord will raise them up; and anyone who has committed sins will be forgiven. Therefore confess your sins to one another, and pray for one another, so that you may be healed. The prayer of the righteous is powerful and effective" (James 5:14–16).

We **commune at the table** where our Lord, with broken loaf, says, "This is my body that is for you. Do this in remembrance of me" (1 Cor 11:24), and, with cup uplifted, says, "This is the cup of the new covenant in my blood" (v 25).

As the **servant people** of God, we wash each other's feet in obedience to our Lord who, after washing the feet of his disciples, said, "So if I, your Lord and Teacher, have washed your feet, you also should do as I have done to you" (John 13:14). All of us are called to the role of servant, for our Lord says, "I have set you an example, that you also should do as I have done to you" (v 15).

We seek to be part of the answer to our Lord's prayer "**that they may all be one**. As you, Father, are in me and I am in you, may they also be in us, so that the world may believe that you have sent me" (John 17:21).

And, with glad hearts, we are earnestly committed to **living out the glorious reality we have in Christ** that "there is no longer Jew or Greek, there is no longer slave or free, there is no longer male and female; for all of you are one in Christ Jesus" (Gal 3:28). We praise God for the grace that makes all who are in Christ, "Abraham's offspring, heirs according to the promise" (v 29). Thanks be to God!

IV. Confessions about the Kingdom

As people **commissioned "to proclaim the kingdom of God and to heal"** (Luke 9:2), we are **committed to ministering in the name of Christ** who, in the words of Isaiah, said, "The Spirit of the Lord is upon me, because he has anointed me to bring good news to the poor. He has sent me to proclaim release to the captives and recovery of sight to the blind, to let the oppressed go free, to proclaim the year of the Lord's favor" (Luke 4:18–19).

As believers, we live in **the present reality of the kingdom**, which is "righteousness and peace and joy in the Holy Spirit" (Rom 14:17).

It is out of devotion to Christ and compassion for the lost that we proclaim the gospel knowing that all of us face **final judgment** at the time of our Lord's return when to those who live in harmony with the kingdom, the Lord says, "Come, you that are blessed by my Father, inherit the kingdom prepared for you from the foundation of the world" (Matt 25:34) but to those who refuse, he says, "Depart from me into the eternal fire prepared for the devil and his angels" (v 41). "And these will go away into eternal punishment, but the righteous into eternal life" (v 46).

As people of the kingdom, we look forward to the one and only **return of the Lord**, when "the Lord himself, with a cry of command, with the archangel's call and with the sound of God's trumpet, will descend from heaven, and the dead in Christ will rise first. Then we who are alive, who are left, will be caught up in the clouds together with them to meet the Lord in the air; and so we will be with the Lord forever" (1 Thess 4:16–17).

Maranatha! "Come, Lord Jesus!" (Rev 22:20).

Celebration of Faith

Prelude: A Medley of Heritage Music
"I'm Redeemed"; "Joy Unspeakable"; "The Family of God"

Call to Worship: Solo "Come Magnify"[2]

*Hymn No. 83: "Once Again We Come"[3]

Confessions about Scripture and about God: Introduction and Part I of "As Christians, Here We Stand"

*Hymn No. 46: "What a Mighty God We Serve!"

*Extemporaneous Prayers of Praise and Thanksgiving

*Hymn No. 567: "A Child of God"

Confessions about Salvation: Part II of "As Christians, Here We Stand"

Musical Group: "It Is by Grace"[4]

2. Words and music by Ken Sifford, in *I Lift My Voice: Songs from the Heart* (Anderson, IN: Church of God Ministries, 2001), 5–6, with guitar sheet on 43. This song is also recorded on the *I Lift My Voice* CD. Copyright ©2001 by Church of God Ministries.
3. All hymn numbers are from *Worship the Lord: Hymnal of the Church of God* (Anderson, IN: Warner Press, 1989).
4. Words and music by Tim Irwin, in *I Lift My Voice*, 21–22, with guitar sheet on 57. Copyright ©2001 by Church of God Ministries.

Salvation Testimonies

Confessions about the Church: Part III of "As Christians, Here We Stand"

Hymn No. 330: "The Bond of Perfectness"

Prayers for the Church Both Here and around the World

Missionary Offering during which the congregation sings hymn no. 297: "Together We Go to Make Disciples"

Confessions about the Kingdom: Part IV of "As Christians, Here We Stand"

*__Hymn No. 690__: "When My King Shall Call for Me"

*__Benediction__

*__Dispersal Song and Postlude__: The congregation sings hymn no. 616, "There Is Joy in the Lord," after which the instrumentalist continues playing as the people disperse.

(*All who are able will please stand.)

Possible Sermon Series on Vision

Possibility 1
Series: "The Church That Pleases God"

The Importance of Being a God-Pleasing Church
> Sermon 1: Revelation 1:9–3:3

A Gospel Church
> Sermon 2: Romans 1:1–17
> Sermon 3: Galatians 1:1–10
> Sermon 4: Ephesians 1

A Bible Church
> Sermon 5: 2 Timothy 3:14–17
> Sermon 6: Luke 24:13–49

A Born-Again Church
> Sermon 7: John 3:1–10
> Sermon 8: 2 Corinthians 5:16–17

A Holiness Church
> Sermon 9: Acts 2:1–4
> Sermon 10: 1 Thessalonians 5:23–24
> Sermon 11: Romans 12:1–2
> Sermon 12: 1 John 4:7–21

A Unity Church
> Sermon 13: John 17:20–26

Sermon 14: 1 Corinthians 12:12–31
Sermon 15: Ephesians 4:1–16

A Kingdom of God Church
Sermons 16 and 17: The Gospel of Matthew
Sermon 18: Luke 9:1–2
Sermon 19: Romans 14:17

A Missionary Church
Sermon 20: Matthew 28:18–21
Sermon 21: Acts 1:8; 2:1–4, 37–47

Possibility 2
Series: As Christians, Here We Stand

The Starting Point
Sermon 1: The Written Word (2 Timothy 2:16–17)
Sermon 2: The Eternal Word (John 1:1–18)

God
Sermon 3: The One God: Father, Son, and Holy Spirit (Deuteronomy 6:4; Matthew 28:19; 1 Corinthians 12:4–6; 2 Corinthians 13:13; Ephesians 4:4–6; 2 Thessalonians 2:13–14; 1 Peter 1:2)
Sermon 4: Jesus Christ (Colossians 1:15–20)
Sermon 5: The Holy Spirit (John 14:15–31; 16:4–15)

Salvation
Sermon 6: Sin and Salvation (Romans 3:23; John 3:16; 2 Corinthians 5:17)
Sermon 7: Baptism (Romans 6:1–11; Acts 2:37–41)
Sermon 8: Pressing On to the Goal (Philippians 3:12–16)
Sermon 9: Being Filled with the Spirit (Ephesians 5:15–20)
Sermon 10: Victory Over Sin (1 John 2:1–2)
Sermon 11: Consecration (Romans 12:1–2)

Sermon 12: Entire Sanctification (1 Thessalonians 5:23–24)
Sermon 13: Perfect Love (1 John 4:17–21)
   Sermon 14: Security as We Abide in Christ (John 10:28; 15:1–11; Matthew 10:22)

Church
Sermon 15: Making Disciples (Matthew 28:19–21)
Sermon 16: The Body of Christ (1 Corinthians 12:27–28)
Sermon 17: The New Humanity (Ephesians 2:11–22)
Sermon 18: The People of God (1 Peter 2:9–10)
Sermon 19: Church Membership (Acts 2:47)
Sermon 20: The Empowered Church (Acts 2)
Sermon 21: The One Church (Ephesians 4:1–7; 1 Corinthians 12:12–13)
Sermon 22: The Gifted Church (1 Corinthians 12:4–11)
Sermon 23: The Reforming Church (Revelation 2:7, 11, 17, 29; 3:6, 13, 22)
Sermon 24: The Gathered Church (Hebrews 10:23–25)
Sermon 25: The Worshiping Church (John 4:24; Acts 2:42; 5:19; Philippians 4:6; 1 Corinthians 11:23–26)
Sermon 26: The Anointing Church (James 5:13–16)
Sermon 27: The Servant Church (John 13:1–20)
Sermon 28: The Reconciled Church (2 Corinthians 5:16–21; Galatians 3:28)

Kingdom
Sermon 29: Our Lord's Ministry (Luke 4:16–21)
Sermon 30: Our Lord's Commission (Luke 9:1–2)
Sermon 31: Our Lord's Reign Now (Ephesians 1:20–23)
Sermon 32: The Essence of Our Lord's Kingdom (Romans 14:17)
Sermon 33: Our Lord's Final Judgment (Matthew 25:31–46)
Sermon 34: Our Lord's Glorious Return (1 Thessalonians 4:13–18)
Sermon 35: Our Lord's Heavenly Reign (Revelation 21:9–22:5)

APPENDIX 4

Statement of Accountability

We submit to Jesus Christ as the Lord of the church and to the Bible as the rule of faith and practice. We affirm the understanding of the Christian faith and the historic vision of the Church of God as set forth in _____
_____.

Furthermore, we request the spiritual oversight of, and, if necessary, the intervention of _____
_____:

To hold the preaching, teaching, and leadership ministry of our congregation accountable to the above, and

To hold the ministerial staff, congregational officers and the corporate structure of our congregation accountable for:

- Good order in business affairs,
- Christian ethics in all relationships,
- Christian morality, and
- Cooperation with the mission and ministry of the Church of God as a whole.

BOOK 3

SIGNALS
at the
CROSSROADS

INTRODUCTION

The Church of God reformation movement has many things to rejoice about, some things to lament, and much hope for the future. The movement no longer lives in the nineteenth or twentieth centuries. What does it mean for the movement to be the church in the twenty-first century? Red, yellow, and green signal lights are at the crossroads. I am convinced that the church will give heed to the red and yellow lights only when it sees lots of green. Without the green, there really is no reason to deal with the red and yellow lights. So this is a book of hope and optimism, a book of honesty and realism, a book of historical rootedness and renewed idealism.

I want this book to serve the same purpose as the first two, namely, to provide a focus for a church-wide conversation about our life together. While not written originally with the idea that it would provide such a focus for the church internationally, I was surprised to find that to be the case. Therefore, I assume that while my target audience is the North American context, this writing also may be of some benefit to the church internationally.

My intention is to celebrate good things that are happening among us, so that the first chapter is entitled, "Hallelujahs at the Crossroads." I would then move on to…a comparison of the church in the nineteenth century and the church in the twenty-first. In this chapter I would develop a perspective on the variety of congregations that make up our life together.[1]

The last four chapters will set forth some ideals for us, the landmarks that guide us, aids for how we go about recognizing the historic Christian church, the Church of God, a twenty-first-century

---

1. Gil Stafford reversed the order of these two chapters when he began writing this volume.

church, and a kingdom church. I would conclude then with "red, yellow, and greens" for us.

It is my intention that this would be a book of encouragement, of challenge, and of theological perspective for the church. I hope that it will contribute beneficially to the health of the church.

Gilbert W. Stafford
Anderson, Indiana
November 19, 2007

CHAPTER 1

Then and Now

I observe that in the Church of God we have at least eight different kinds of congregations: the local down-home church, the headquarters church, the tightly controlled ethnic church, the independent smaller church, the disconnected larger church, the originalist church, the theologically divergent church, and the emergent connectional church.

The local down-home church is a congregation that has a well-established way of being church that is comfortable to its members. It is unsophisticated in its relationship to the wider church, whether Church of God or otherwise. It is not particularly antagonistic to the wider church, but its concerns are not particularly theirs. The most important consideration is the comfort level of its people. They enjoy being with each other, and if others come along and are comfortable with what they enjoy and the way they do things and will not rock the boat, they will embrace them into the circle. But it is very clear that this is "our church" and that things will stay the way they are for as long as they are comfortable with them. Church is merely a slightly more public form of home life.

The headquarters church is a congregation that considers itself to be connected with the national and international ministries of the church with national offices in Anderson, Indiana. The people think of themselves as linked to the wider Church of God and find pleasure in "our worldwide ministries." The church looks for leadership to state, area, and national agencies and organizations. It participates programmatically and budgetarily in the state and national work of the church. Its members can be counted on to be present in district, state, and national meetings. Their sense of identity is merged with the whole life of the church. Indeed, they consider themselves to be a local expression of the Church of God as a whole. They cherish the history and traditions of the Church of God movement.

The tightly controlled ethnic church is a congregation that finds its basic identity in its ethnicity, such as German, Hispanic, African American, Anglo. It is convinced that its ethnic make-up must be preserved in order for the church to be in health. Ethnicity issues trump theological considerations. It may either draw lines of demarcation whereby persons of other ethnic groups are effectively kept out (as for example, by the use of the ethnic language only or by overt refusal to accept persons who are different or by cold treatment), or it may be willing to accept outsiders as long as they are willing to embrace the ethnicity of the church. The tightly controlled ethnic church is convinced that it is important to preserve its cultural way of being church and that to lose it is to lose a cultural heritage that is considered to be the most important value of that congregation. Its sense of identity is more with congregations and organizations of the same ethnicity than it is with the wider church. It measures all fellowship and cooperation with the wider church on the basis of whether it endangers its ethnicity.

The independent church is a congregation that is forthright in its stance that it and it alone decides what happens in its church. This independence may be grounded in a theological understanding regarding the autonomy of the local congregation. The congregation has nothing to do with other Church of God congregations, even those close by. It attends no district, state, or national meetings. It views listing in the *Yearbook of the Church of God* as a nuisance. It smarts at mailings from state or national offices. They end up in the trash can. Cooperation is not in its vocabulary. It may have some associational life with other independent smaller churches that share the same theological stance regarding local independence, but that associational life does not spill over into its relationships with other Church of God congregations that do not share that theological stance. These churches are a world unto themselves, convinced that the way they do things is the right way and that the wider church is a threat to their independence.

The disconnected church is a congregation that has been numerically successful, or hopes to be, and finds that its membership has so few people with a Church of God identity that to stress Church of God connections would be meaningless and probably harmful. A visitor would find it difficult, if not impossible, to find any sign of linkage with the Church of God. Indeed, longer term members would find it surprising if someone were to tell them that it is a congregation of the Church of God. Listing in the *Yearbook of the Church of God* is a nuisance. Its associational life is primarily with other kinds of organizations that share their same growth and programmatic commitments. It does not have the time or energy to expend on district, state, regional, and national organizations and endeavors. Indeed, it views these as defunct, ineffective, and demoralizing. Its disconnection is the result of practical considerations rather than theology.

The originalist church is a congregation that wants to toe the line in relation to the early doctrine and practices of the Church of God. It is convinced that much of the church has lost touch with the heritage of the Church of God, and it views its mission as that of keeping alive the heritage. The old ways are the best ways. The literature of the early days is the standard by which everything is to be measured. Originalist churches are concerned with purity of doctrine and practice. They are reticent to question the tradition; indeed, they look askance at those who do so. The originalist church finds fellowship with other originalist churches and is convinced that God uses it to witness to the wider church that has veered off the track, regarding the purity of doctrine and practice. The originalist church loves the whole church but fears for its future. It hopes that the wider church wakes up before the divinely inspired tradition is completely lost in the Church of God.

The theologically divergent church is a congregation that holds a doctrinal position very different from the historical doctrinal positions of the Church of God. These doctrinal positions are enunciated publicly and are part and parcel of the local identity. Examples are congregations that are, for all practical purposes, conservative Baptist or Pentecostal in theological orientation. Examples of issues that set them apart from the historic positions of the Church of God are the rejection of women in ministry; the charismatic phenomena that are stressed by Pentecostals, such as tongues speaking and being slain in the Spirit; the eternal security of persons who at some point made a decision for Christ, regardless of their subsequent life; premillennialism; and the fourfold hierarchy of ministry based on Ephesians 4: 11 regarding apostles, prophets, evangelists, and pastors and teachers.

The emergent connectional church is a congregation that is experimenting with new forms of organization, worship, and methodology but is doing so in close connection with the wider Church of God. While its identity as a Church of God congregation is not in the foreground of its public image, it does not seek to hide the fact that its root system is in the Church of God. It keeps its leadership connected with the wider Church of God. It offers its resources for the benefit of the Church of God. It is cooperative in the district, state, regional, national, and international work of the Church of God. Its theological stance is in harmony with historic Church of God understandings and practices. It has built into its organizational structures safeguards that the congregation will remain committed to the Church of God even after the days of current leadership are over.

❧

As I reflect on the Church of God movement in the nineteenth century and the movement in the twenty-first century, I see some major shifts. These include a shift away from accusation to affirmation; a shift from "come out" to "entering into"; a shift from polemics to hospitality; a shift from pride of truth to humility in truth; and a shift from "us and them" to "we."

The early literature of the Church of God is filled with accusations about those who were in denominations. They were in Babylon. The denominational system was held up to ridicule. Steeple-churches were places of dead spirituality. One looks with no success to find any words of appreciation for the work and witness of other church groups. That has changed, for the most part, in the twenty-first century. We affirm what God is doing in the wider church. We rejoice wherever we see evidence of the presence of the kingdom. We take pleasure in the life transformation that we witness taking place in other church groups. Instead of pointing a finger of accusation, we offer hands of blessing for what God is doing in other parts of his household.

We once were tagged as the "come-outers" because our only approach to the practice of Christian unity was to call people to "come out from among them and be ye separate." What we meant was to come out from the denominational system and come to us, where they could find liberty to enjoy the freedom of the children of God unfettered by denominational rules, regulations, organizations, and statements of faith. In the twenty-first-century, one hears less and less about coming out; now the emphasis is more on entering into the life of the wider church, not only for the purpose of sharing the insights and perspectives that we are so convinced are biblical and that the rest of the church would benefit from, but also for the purpose of being enriched by the wider church. The more operative idea now is that God's grace is manifold, that the riches of his truth are so great that no one tradition of the Christian faith can possibly contain it all, and that we all need to be enriched by those of the faith who are equally devoted to Christ and to the teachings of Scripture.

We have moved from the nineteenth-century emphasis on polemics to a twenty-first-century emphasis on hospitality. Whereas
it used to be that we were ready to take anybody on for the sake
of proving them wrong and us right, we now are a kinder, gentler,
more hospitable generation of saints. I remember as a boy at my
grandparent's house arguing into the night with my Baptist cousin
that the Church of God was the oldest church. My Church of God
grandparents listened with delight as I took on my cousin. It was as
though they were applauding me, hoping that the Church of God
side would win and that my poor Baptist cousin would go down in
defeat. (I was always bothered by the fact that he never pulled the
covers over his head in defeat but kept smiling on into the night!)
I was, indeed, a child of the movement. How different things are
now: I am hospitable to my Roman Catholic, Baptist, and Presbyterian cousins. We no longer get into polemical arguments. Now
it is a matter of learning from each other, explaining to each other,
and sharing with each other. I think that what has happened to me
from the time of my early teen-age years to now is a reflection of
what has happened generally in the whole movement.

There is among us a change from an attitude of pride in truth
to an attitude of humility in truth. Truth is still important among
us. But what a difference there is between those who take pride in
having it all put together and who think it's too bad that others
are either not smart enough or spiritual enough to see it and those
who are humble in their understanding of the truth, knowing that
the way we state the truth may need further clarification, that our
understanding of the truth itself may need to be revised in light
of further evidence, or that others may have dimensions of truth
that would enhance our own understanding. What a difference
there is between these two attitudes! The pride of truth brings a
harsh smirk to the face; humility in truth brings a gentle smile.
Pride of truth has only one's own podium from which to speak;
humility of truth shares the podium along with comfortable chairs
for further conversation.

In the nineteenth century, the church experience was clearly
an "us and them" world, whereas now it is a "we" world. They

were the enemy of God; we were the chosen of God. As a result, they were our enemies too. The twenty-first century sees among us more of a "we are in this thing together" approach. The world out of kilter with the plans of God is the common enemy. Sin is the common enemy. Demonic forces at work in our world are the common enemy. Yes, different traditions of Christian faith have different perspectives, different approaches, different emphases, different understanding, but nevertheless we are people of the one and only Lord Jesus Christ. We are in the same faith boat. Many factors have brought this about: Our world is smaller, so we know each other better. Intermarriage means that it isn't very easy to think of one's children who love the Lord but who marry individuals of other Christian traditions and participate in those traditions as the enemy. And the ecumenical movement has led to cooperative efforts nationally and locally, interchurch networking in which we share all kinds of resources with each other. Most, but certainly not all, of the Christian church in the twenty-first century is in the "we" mode rather than the "us and them" mode. Most, certainly not all, of the Church of God is in the "we" mode.

The twenty-first century is not the nineteenth!

CHAPTER 2

Twenty Hallelujahs at the Crossroads

1. Hallelujah for Sustaining Health and Pastoral Excellence.
Thanks to a grant of some 1.7 million dollars from the Lilly Endowment, the Church of God has been able to develop a network of pastoral relationships called SHAPE (Sustaining Health and Pastoral Excellence). Pastors enter into a three-year commitment to a cluster of other pastors. Since its beginning in 2002 some five hundred fifty pastors and state leaders have finished or begun their three-year covenant. SHAPE is now a reality in some fourteen regions covering fifteen states. As a result, pastors are being led out of isolation into greater connectivity; they are discovering new resources for their ministries; they are finding a safe place to process what is going on in their lives and ministries; they are finding the opportunity to understand different perspectives among Church of God pastors. Pastors in SHAPE are experiencing a renewed sense of vocational calling.

The Church of God endeavor has been so successful that Lilly made a second grant for the further development of SHAPE-like experiences among ministerial students in our colleges, universities, and seminary. Leaders of these institutions of higher learning have met to develop a strategy for making this happen. The goal is that the SHAPE experience will become a way of life for Church of God ministers from the point of entry into ministry all the way into the future of one's ministry.

The assumption is that healthy pastors contribute significantly to the health of local churches, and healthy congregations contribute to the health of communities. This, then, is a first major step toward the church impacting the culture in the best possible way for the sake of the kingdom.

John Wimmer, program director with Lilly Endowment, on August 22, 2007, wrote to Dr. Ronald Duncan of Church of God Ministries: "I celebrate with you the signs of change you are seeing throughout the Church of God (Anderson) movement, especially the new sense of connectedness, not just among pastors but throughout the movement. I think it is great that SHAPE is challenging you to reflect so deeply on what it means to be a holiness movement...."

Hallelujah! Something mighty good is happening to Church of God pastors! And to our churches and to the culture! The Church of God is helping to point the way.

2. Hallelujah for the new associational life among the regional pastors and overseers.

One of the remarkable developments of the last decade or so has been the development of stronger leadership among regional pastors and overseers. As of 2008, there are about thirty-three state or area assemblies that have area administrators. They meet twice a year and as a group have officers. This gives them the opportunity to develop common goals, procedures, and philosophy about their role in the life of the church. They can deal with issues having to do with credentialing and the movement of ministers from one state or area to another. These persons have their hands on the pulse of the church in their respective areas, which means that when they share with each other as a group there is the golden opportunity to identify trends, challenges, and victories for the church at large.

The titles given to these persons by the respective areas are an indication of the church's desire regarding the role of these individuals: executive minister, executive director, district coordinator, conference pastor, state pastor, area administrator, state minister, executive state minister, director of ministries, state pastor and overseer, state administrator, executive coordinator, director of ministries, district administrator, state ministries pastor, and executive director of ministry services. Combining these sixteen different designations, one sees the following eight broad designations: executive minister, executive director, coordinator, pastor, administrator, minister, director of ministries, and overseer. Two conceptual groupings emerge: (1) executive, administrator, director, coordinator, and overseer; and (2) minister, pastor. The first terminology is oriented more toward chief operating officer; the second has more of a shepherding orientation. The tendency is in the direction of strong leadership at the area level.

Hallelujah! There is a new awareness among our congregations that we must be good stewards of our life together.

3. Hallelujah for the model of the building blocks of message, mission, ministry, and methods developed by Church of God Ministries for our work together.

So often in the life of the church we get the cart before the horse. We talk about *methods* of doing ministry without any serious consideration being given to what it is that we are about. Sometimes we function in the life of the church like an unwise builder who puts up a building without knowing what its purpose is: Is it a house? For whom? What kind of life do they want to have? Or, is it a store? What do they want to sell? Does anyone want it?

Voices in Church of God Ministries are saying with great clarity, first of all we have to clarify what our message is. Then and only then will we be in a position to talk meaningfully about our mission as a movement. That message/mission should determine the ministries we have. Once the message/mission/ministries are clarified, only then are we ready to develop methods of going about ministry. Otherwise, we are just spinning our institutional wheels. Message leads to mission, which leads to ministries, which in turn leads to methods. This principle applies not only to the national offices; it applies to area work and to local congregational life. What is the message that Fairview Church of God in Falkville, Alabama, has for people in general in that area of North Alabama and for the whole Christian community in that place? What is its mission under God? What are the ministries that are appropriate to its message/mission? And what methods will Fairview Church use in order to do its ministries in order to most effectively share its message and accomplish its mission? Fairview Church of God in Falkville as well as Church of God Ministries needs to function with these building blocks in place, and in the right order: message, mission, ministries, and then methods.

Hallelujah! Many among us *are* getting the horse before the cart.

4. Hallelujah for the entrepreneurial spirit among us.

In 2006, First Church of God in Bristow, Oklahoma, was getting ready to celebrate their centennial. They wanted my father, a former pastor, to come back for the celebration, but due to health matters he wasn't able to go, so they invited me instead. As I prepared to go, I asked him what he remembered about his pastorate there that he would like for me to share with them. He told about times when he wanted to do things but because of a concern about the possibility of the church overextending itself financially he would put on the brakes. But, he said, there was always a man on the board of trustees who would inevitably say: "But pastor, we *can* do it; we can *do it*." Dad told that story over and over, and referred to him as the "can-do man."

That is one of the wonderful characteristics of the Church of God; it is filled with "can do people." If one were to take a look at the section in the *Yearbook of the Church of God*, titled "Freestanding Ministry Organizations" one would find a list of organizations that have emerged from the life of the church. It is the church saying, we can do something about providing medicines and medical materials in places of great need throughout the world. We can do something concrete about the elimination of racism and violence. We can do something about ministering to street people. We can do something about families living below the poverty level, those affected by incarceration, and those suffering from abuse. We can do something about giving urban youth tools for success on the right side of life. We can do something about the AIDS crisis in Africa. We can do something about increasing the level of prayer commitment among the people of God. We can do something about ministry to the deaf. We can do something about bringing

Christian laypeople from across the nation to local congregations to bless and encourage growth in Christ. On and on the list goes. None of these endeavors started within the formal structures of our state or national offices. All of them emerged because the people of God said, "Something needs to be done about this, and by God's grace we are going to do something about it." This list of organizations and ministries does not fit neatly into an organization flow chart. It is simply the people of God serving as divine entrepreneurs for the sake of the kingdom.

Hallelujah! The can-do spirit is alive and well among us!

5. Hallelujah that we are on the other side of financial disasters. For far too many years, our life has been cluttered by financial crises and disasters with which we as a whole had little or nothing to do, and yet when the disaster struck, it was as though the problem belonged to all of us to solve. Far too many sessions in the General Assembly of the Church of God over the recent decades have been dominated by these financial disasters. Getting on with the mission of the church was hampered by survival techniques, institutional face-saving endeavors, dealing with decisions made by boards that did not have the counsel of the whole church. And yet when the financial mess took place, the counsel of the whole church was needed, as were its resources. Enough is enough of that sort of thing. May it never happen again! For the first time in too long, we are coming up for air and talking about life on the other side of these financial disasters. New policies of accountability are in place. Now it is a matter of getting our resources together to pursue our mission with the ministries to which God has called us.

Hallelujah! We have no financial disasters to distract us from kingdom work!

6. Hallelujah for the new positive, cooperative relationship between our schools of higher education.
What a wonderful sight it was in a recent General Assembly of the Church of God to see the presidents of our colleges and

universities standing as a unit before the Assembly making a joint statement about Christian higher education in the Church of God. These presidents give every indication of genuinely appreciating each other. They recognize that each of the schools has a distinct role to play in the life of the church and that the church needs all of them. Meanspirited competition is absent. It must have been the hand of the Lord—it certainly was not because we had a grand plan—that we have four healthy liberal arts schools scattered across the United States, in Oregon, Indiana, Oklahoma, and Florida.

It is also a blessing that these four schools join with the leaders of other schools from throughout the world for an annual meeting in which they explore ways they can all be mutually supportive of the education endeavor of the Church of God around the world.

Hallelujah! Sweet camaraderie is the order of the day among our schools of higher education, both in the United States and around the world!

7. Hallelujah for the new models of congregational life springing up across the country.

We have quite a few congregations that are developing new models of congregational life in relation to organizational structure: they are simplifying their organizational life so that life and ministry does not get squeezed out by bureaucratic processes. These new organizational structures correct the idea that serving on committees and boards is the way to be involved in ministry. They place the focus on *actual ministry* rather than on merely *plans about ministry*.

Other new models of congregational life are developing in relation to how the congregation impacts the culture for the sake of the kingdom. These new models take into consideration the fact that the culture is constantly changing and, therefore, a congregation that is effective in impacting the culture has to be constantly changing its ways of making an impact. The contemporary culture is different than it was even five years ago—new issues, new challenges, new influences, new local, national, and international realities are part and parcel of our culture today that five years ago were nonexistent. It is today's culture that the church is called on to impact for the sake of the kingdom, not the culture of yesterday. Some of our congregations are very much in touch with this reality and are functioning accordingly.

Still other models are developing that take into account the importance of the local church being a covenant community instead of merely a collection of individuals who for whatever reason end up in one place for a while. What responsibility does each person in the congregation have to the well-being of the whole community of faith? What responsibility does the community of faith have toward the individual person? What lines of accountability are needed in order for the church to function as a wholesome unit rather than as a collection of individuals each doing his or her own thing quite independently of any consideration of the whole?

Hallelujah! We have an encouraging number of congregations that are being creative in the development of new ways of being church for the sake of the kingdom. May the number continue to increase!

8. Hallelujah for the immediacy of response made by compassionate ministries to crises.[1]

9. Hallelujah for membership in Christian Churches Together in the USA as well as in other interchurch and ecumenical organizations.

10. Hallelujah for a theological wholeness with a strong historical root system.

11. Hallelujah for emphasis on youth and the benefit of the youthful spirit.

---

1. Editor's Note: Here Dr. Stafford lists the other Church of God trends that he believed were cause for rejoicing. However, his final illness prevented him from writing further comments about them.

244

12. Hallelujah for a renewed emphasis on our historical root system.

13. Hallelujah for a singing church with a cherished musical tradition.

14. Hallelujah for emphasis on personal holiness along with social justice.

15. Hallelujah for programs that are in place to equip ministers at whatever level: Center for Christian Leadership; undergraduate programs; graduate programs; doctoral program.

16. Hallelujah for the hospice of dying congregations and the opportunities for using those resources to relaunch ministries.

17. Hallelujah for a commitment to the struggles with interracial, intercultural, and gender-related issues.

18. Hallelujah for new financial resources for church planting.

19. Hallelujah for creative tension between the creative impulse and mature stability.

20. Hallelujah for movement in the direction of standardization of credentialing of ministers.

AFTERWORD

"You Shall Be Holy for I Am Holy"

(Dr. Stafford's last chapel address at the Anderson University School of Theology, delivered November 27, 2007)

The word *holy* is so much a part of the biblical text, yet the word has been secularized. When we speak of someone who is afflicted with hypocrisy, we say they have a "holier-than-thou" attitude. Or if we're talking about an idea or practice that we don't touch, we call it a "sacred cow" or a "holy cow." A long time ago, there was a radio and television series called *Amos 'n' Andy* in which Amos used to exclaim, "Holy mackerel!" We often say, "Holy baloney," "Holy smokes," and so on. When a word like *holy* is used casually like that, is its original meaning retrievable?

The word *holy* appears often in our hymnody. We used it this morning in our songs and choruses. That is appropriate, for the word *holy* is used extensively throughout the whole of Scripture.

You will recall the passage in Isaiah 6 where Isaiah the prophet tells us about visiting the temple and seeing Lord sitting on a throne, "high and lifted up." Then in verse 3, Isaiah hears the heavenly creatures calling out,

> Holy, holy, holy is the LORD God of hosts.
> Heaven and earth are full of his glory.

In the midst of that overwhelming experience of the holiness of God, Isaiah laments his own spiritual neediness. "Woe is me! I am lost. I am a man of unclean lips."

Then notice what happens. One of the heavenly creatures flies to Isaiah with a live coal that is taken from the altar with a pair of tongs. It touches his mouth, saying, "Now that this has touched your lips, your guilt has departed and your sin is blotted out."

In verse 8, Isaiah hears the voice of the Lord saying, "Whom shall I send, and who will go for us?" Then Isaiah says, "Here am I. Send me." If you follow along in verse 9, the Lord tells him to go, and gives him specific instructions about his divine mission.

So Isaiah 6 describes a holy God who has a mission, and he calls Isaiah into that divine mission. In this one frame of Scripture, we see what biblical holiness is all about. It is about the holy God preparing us and sending us on mission. Holiness is about our entering, by the grace and power of God, into the divine mission.

As we look at the rest of the biblical record, what else do we discover about the holiness of God?

For one thing, we can say that he is the one and only living God. All other gods are created by human ingenuity. Only the biblical God has brought us into existence so that we can serve his purposes. There is only one living God. That's what it means to be the holy God.

To be the holy God means that he is awe-inspiring. We find ourselves wilting in the presence of his glory. It's one thing to enjoy singing about his holiness, quite another thing to be wilting in the presence of his majesty. But that's what Scripture means when it says God is holy. He is awe-inspiring.

When Scripture says that God is holy, it means that he is beyond human manageability. He is no lucky charm. It is impossible to control him. He holds the final outcome of human history. And what is that final outcome? Jesus Christ is the final outcome—we already know where history is going. It is consummated in Jesus Christ. That's what the whole book of Revelation is about, isn't it? As we look at the ins and outs of human history, we sometimes wonder, Where is all this going? While in the interim it may appear that God has lost control, we see in the life, death, and resurrection of Jesus Christ that God has won. We live in the glory of his victory even now. That's what the Bible means when it says God is holy: the outcome is guaranteed.

When the Bible says that God is holy, it means that God is jealous about our well-being. God is like a jealous parent who will not tolerate the violation of his son or his daughter. If your child is violated, it's no time to be "nice." If your spouse is violated, it's no time to be "nice." So when God's children are violated, God is not "nice."

When the Bible says that God is holy, it means that God is on mission to accomplish his goals and his purposes. This biblical God is not a passive, withdrawn, introverted god. He is a mission-oriented God; he is an activist God; he is a purpose-driven God. We may think of God as a self-centered deity, drawing all the universe's energy of adoration to himself, but God is not a vacuum-sweeper god. Instead he is a bow-and-arrow God, who has a target toward which all of his energies are gathered. He is not an energy-sucking god, but an energy-radiating God.

I remind you of the phrase found throughout Scripture that refers to "the Lord of hosts." I have a new appreciation for that phrase. It means that all of heaven's spiritual resources are at his fingertips. So when "the Lord of hosts" acts, he brings together all of heaven's army, all of heaven's energy, to accomplish his purposes. Oh, it's wonderful to have "the Lord of hosts" on your side!

Now the stage is set for understanding 1 Peter 1:15–16, which was read awhile ago: "As he who called you is holy, be holy yourselves in all your conduct; for it is written, 'You shall be holy, for I am holy.'" As people of the holy God, we are to be holy people. What does that mean? Does it mean that we are flawless? Does it mean that we are little gods? Does it mean that we are withdrawn from the world? Does it mean that we are disengaged from life? Does it mean that we are ceramic dolls in a display case?

No to all. For us to be the holy people of the holy God means that we are devoted wholeheartedly to the one and only living God. With all of the gods of the world surrounding us, how can we possibly be wholeheartedly devoted to him? How can that be? The answer is found in two words.

One is *yield*. We must yield to him. He calls; we answer in faith. That's what Mary, the mother of our Lord, did when the angel appeared to her. Her answer was, "Here am I, the servant of the Lord." That's what Simon and Andrew did when Jesus called them to fish for people. "Immediately, they left their nets and followed him." That's what Paul did on the road to Damascus. He "stopped kicking against the pricks" and he yielded. That's what Lydia did when the Lord opened her heart to hear the message of Paul; she yielded to it.

We have a lot of good holiness literature about yielding. We even have places where you can publicly yield to God. You can come to this altar and you can yield. I've done it; you've done it. We can't be the holy people of God without yielding to him. "Is your all on the altar?," the hymn asks. Have you yielded?

Yet sometimes we miss the second word, which is *avail*. Perhaps we know how to yield, yield, yield, yield, but have we availed ourselves of God's resources to be his holy people?

There are so many resources in Scripture. One is the sign of baptism, described in Romans 6. The sign of baptism over your life reminds you how you are to live every day: Dead to sin, alive to God. Did you get up this morning and avail yourself of the sign of your baptism?

Another resource is the presence of the Holy Spirit. Sometimes we begin the Christian life and it becomes a kind of "works righteousness," because we do not avail ourselves of the empowerment of the Holy Spirit, the guidance of the Spirit, the counsel of the Spirit.

Avail yourself of the written Word of God. I just finished reading the letters of Dietrich Bonhoeffer in prison, and I was reminded again of how important the written Word was every day to him. He was sharing with other people outside the prison that it gave him guidance and courage through those dark, dark days. The written Word of God is the definitive "hard copy" of God's message to us. Avail yourself of the Word.

Have you availed yourself of the Lord's Table, where we commune with the Lord and claim his saving grace? We had such a marvelous time of Communion in our church on Sunday night. For about twenty or twenty-five minutes, we were there at the Table of the Lord. How precious that time, when the Lord's strength was given us! Perspective and insight were gained at the Table of the Lord. We don't celebrate a dead Lord, but we commune with a risen, living Lord, availing ourselves of the riches of his Table.

Avail yourself of the footwashing position of our Lord, putting yourself in the same position. We can't quite see the face of Jesus until we get in the same position as Jesus.

There's prayer—the never-ending access we have to the Lord, so full of grace—and the sacred assembly, worshiping with the people of God. All of these are the resources that God has made available to us. As we avail ourselves of these wonderful resources, we learn to live as the holy people of God.

So the nature of our holiness is that of coming into conformity with the mission of God, and availing ourselves of all the resources of God so that we can be on mission for him.

I was talking with Dr. Worthington some time ago about the issues in this message, and he reminded me of someone he met recently who said that people in the Old Testament were made unholy for divine service by touching damaged or impure things. For example, lepers; if you touched them, you became unholy. In the New Testament, however, it is by touching damaged and polluted things in the name of Christ that believers demonstrated their divine mission. In Christ, the tables are turned. "Don't touch!" is transformed into, "Do touch—for the sake of the mission."

Holiness gets us dirty. In the terms of the New Testament, to be holy is to take up our cross and follow Jesus. The cross is dirty. It means that we feed the hungry, give water to the thirsty, welcome the stranger, clothe the naked, and visit the sick. That's dirty work. It means that we are empowered by the Spirit to go on foot for Jesus, going into all the world in the name of Jesus, and disciples' feet get dirty in the process. Being the holy people of God is not to be unplugged from the world; it's to be plugged into the divine mission in the world.

Gloria Cumming was a longtime resident of Anderson, a single woman, bashful and of limited financial resources. But Gloria was devoted to writing letters to missionaries around the world. When those missionaries came to Anderson, her home was always a place of hospitality for them, and she invited others in so that they could learn about God's mission around the world. This retiring woman was nonetheless "plugged in" to the divine mission in the world. That's what holiness is.

For the past thirty-two years, I have been privileged to know person after person who has come to seminary at great personal sacrifice and, after graduation, to serve the Lord at great personal sacrifice. I'm reminded of a couple who sold their house, boat, and cars, gave up lucrative careers, and came here to live in a basement apartment where the ceiling was too low for the husband to stand up straight. An apartment with no windows. And then they went to a small, struggling church because they were convinced that it was their divine call. Whenever I talk with them, they tell me about the new things they are doing for the sake of the kingdom.

No, God doesn't call us to be "unplugged" from the world but to get "plugged in" to the divine mission. That's what holiness is.

Take my life and let it be consecrated, Lord, to Thee.
Take my hands and let them move at the impulse of Thy love.
Take my feet and let them be swift and beautiful for Thee.
Take my voice and let me sing always, only for my King.
Take my lips and let them be filled with messages from Thee.
Take my silver and my gold, not a mite would I withhold.
Take my love, my Lord, I pour at Thy feet its treasure store.
Take myself and I will be ever, only, all for Thee. Amen.[1]

---

1. Francis R. Havergal, "Take My Life and Let It Be Consecrated," *Worship the Lord*, 470.

CPSIA information can be obtained at www.ICGtesting.com
Printed in the USA
LVOW101932200313

325082LV00003B/3/P

9 781593 175443